REALISM IN THE DRAMA

T0371281

REALISM IN THE DRAMA

BY

HUGH SYKES DAVIES

Fellow of St John's College

THE LE BAS PRIZE ESSAY 1933

CAMBRIDGE

AT THE UNIVERSITY PRESS

1934

CAMBRIDGE
UNIVERSITY PRESS

University Printing House, Cambridge CB2 8BS, United Kingdom

Cambridge University Press is part of the University of Cambridge.

It furthers the University's mission by disseminating knowledge in the pursuit of education, learning and research at the highest international levels of excellence.

www.cambridge.org
Information on this title: www.cambridge.org/9781107692381

© Cambridge University Press 1934

First published 1934
First paperback edition 2014

A catalogue record for this publication is available from the British Library

ISBN 978-1-107-69238-1 Paperback

CONTENTS

CHAPTER I

INTRODUCTION

THE GENERAL RELATION BETWEEN ART AND CRITICISM: LIMITATIONS OF FORM: METHOD OF THE ESSAY

THE interests of the creative artist and of the critic are fortunately often the same. Conditions of culture and society which benefit the one, will benefit the other, and the bad days of art will be bad days for criticism too. But there is one way at least in which their interests diverge, and it happens that this divergence becomes most apparent when one considers a set subject, such as this of "Realism in the Drama". The divergence is this. The critic's aim is to make himself clear, both to himself, and to others, to arrange his impressions and theories about art in an orderly way; and so he will wish to be clear above all about the meanings of words, of technical terms such as "realism" and "drama". The artist, on the other hand, is concerned with such definitions not at all. He is to express himself not in a rational way, but in any way which happens to occur to him, and the definitions are often a hindrance to such free expressions. There are many writers, for example, who, if they had not decided to be writers, to accept the definition of literature, and to model themselves upon it, would find themselves happier in painting or music, and many painters and musicians who would express themselves better in some form of literature. To this extent, even the most general notions of the arts may become an obstacle to free expression. Though at the same time it must be recognised that the task of the artist might be even harder if he had no such notions to guide him. And the same is true of the minor notions of the more particular forms of expression in each art, such as "the epic", "the pastoral", "the ode", "landscape painting", "still-life", "the sonata", "the symphony". All these are set forms of expression which may hinder or help the artist. And obviously, they are on the whole more likely to help him if they are not too definite, if they do not prescribe with great exactitude what is expected of him, and more likely to hinder him if they are defined with great rigidity. The critic, on the other hand, prefers the definitions to be as rigid as possible, because in this way his own work is made easier, his results are made to seem more valuable. Thus in the eighteenth century, when forms were more sharply defined than at any other period, the critics, such as Boileau and Johnson, could pretend to a finality in their judgments which is absent from the decisions of critics of the less dogmatic periods, such as our own. Johnson was able to dismiss *Lycidas* more easily than any modern critic could dismiss a poem which he disliked: "Its form is that of a pastoral, easy, vulgar, and therefore disgusting: whatever images it can supply are long ago exhausted; and its inherent improbability always forces dissatisfaction on the mind". In just the same way, he is able to bestow very certain praises on *Paradise Lost*: "By the general consent of criticks, the first praise is due to the writer of an epick poem...", Milton, then, has this praise; further, "Bossu is of opinion that the poet's first work is to find a *moral*, which his fable is afterwards to illustrate and establish. This seems to have been the process only of Milton; the moral of other poems is incidental and consequent; in Milton's only it is essential and intrinsick". In this we see the advantages for the critic in the strict definition of terms such as "pastoral" and "epic". And in the poetry of the same period

[3]   1-2

we see the corresponding disadvantages for the poet, in the various *Eclogues* of the eighteenth century, of which those of Collins may be an example, and in the dreary epics made in France.

There are some artists, of course, who are able to adapt their personality to a set form of expression so easily that their work suffers not at all, and even gains by the process. We shall have to consider one or two cases of this kind later. But for the most part, our generalisation is true, that the interests of the artist and of the critic diverge in respect of the clarity of definition of the forms of expression.

From this point of view, the history of art, or of any particular art, may be regarded as a conflict between the critics, trying always to define the forms of art on the evidence of past productions, and the artists themselves, who always tend to overleap the present definitions of the critics, and to find new forms of expression corresponding to their own needs, which, in turn, become part of the definitions of later critics, and serve to hinder artists who come after them. I do not say that this is the only way of regarding the history of art, or that it is even a true statement of the view which I have in mind, but it will serve us

[4]

as a first approximation, to be modified as we like later.

The first conclusions which I wish to draw from it concern the method by which our examination of realism in the drama will be conducted. In the first place, it will explain my unwillingness to give even a rough general definition of realism. Any such definition will have the disadvantage that it is critical, arbitrary, and only vaguely related to the particular artistic problems and solutions which produce this type of work; and it is very much better to avoid giving such definitions at all. On the other hand, I do not mean to leave my readers in the dark about realism. Only, our method of defining it will necessarily follow from the point of view which we have adopted: it will be historical, will be less a definition than a discussion of past definitions, and of works which may be supposed to exhibit more or less faithfully the principles of realism in the drama. And the scheme of this historical examination will be based on our notion of the conflict between the artist and the critic, between the free expression and the forms to which it is, more or less successfully, adapted.

CHAPTER II

THE GREEK DRAMA

I. THEORY

THERE is, of course, only one theorist of the Greek drama—Aristotle. The critical work of the sophists, of Plato, and of Aristophanes, is directed entirely towards the moral, extra-literary aspects of the drama, and does not come within the limits of dramatic criticism.

It is hardly necessary to repeat the accepted commendations of Aristotle's work in full. It will be obvious throughout this essay, as in any work which deals with the drama, that Aristotle's analysis of the plays of the Greeks brought to light, and named all the essential parts of the drama, and that he said things about them which can hardly be improved upon to-day. We shall talk of the "plot", the "characters", the "diction", and so forth, in very much the same way that Aristotle talked of them, and the fact that we put a different emphasis on them, and disagree with him about their relative importance, in no way diminishes our debt to him.

Aristotle, of course, nowhere mentions "realism" in any sense at all. But he lays down doctrines concerning the relation of drama to real life which are extremely relevant to our purpose. We shall find it convenient to distinguish among them a general doctrine, and certain particular doctrines which apply to the management of plot, character, and diction. First, the general doctrine—this is announced in the well-known passage of the *Poetics*: "From what we have said it will be seen that the poet's function is to describe, not the thing that has happened, but a kind of thing that might happen, i.e. what is possible as being probable or necessary".[1] A little later, a significant proviso is added: "And if he (*sc.* the poet) should come to take a subject from actual history, he is none the less a poet for that; since some historic occurrences may very well be in the probable and possible order of things; and it is in that aspect of them that he is their poet".[2]

In the first of these quotations, we have as good a definition of realism in its most general sense as we are likely to find anywhere. In effect, Aristotle points out that nothing should be

[1] The Oxford translation, ch. 9.   [2] *Ibid.*

[7]

represented on the stage which is not a possible occurrence according to the standards which each man forms for himself from his daily experience. This is, let us admit at once, an exceedingly general statement, perhaps so general that it is not likely to be of much use to us in a specific way. But at least it serves to raise the whole question of dramatic illusion, which must necessarily occupy our attention in the following pages. And on this question of dramatic illusion, we may note at once, that Aristotle considers the illusion to be attainable only by submitting the plot to the probabilities of daily life. Obviously a difficulty of practice arises from such a theory. For in the drama of the Greeks, upon which Aristotle's theory was based, it is not uncommon for a god to take human shape, to appear among men, and to play a most important part in the action. Is this in accordance with the probabilities of daily life? We shall consider this question more fully in the second part of this chapter, but for the moment we may note that the answer to it is adumbrated in the second quotation which we have given; anything that *has* happened is possible (otherwise it could not have happened), and the plots of many of the tragedies are historical.

That is to say, the standard of probability to which they refer is in the past, and is not to be refuted by any reference to the present. Thus we may expect to find that in the course of our discussion we shall be compelled to consider the case of the so-called historical, or chronicle play, as a special, or even as a general type of realism, unless we can find some good reason for placing it in another category.

So much, then, for the most general principle of realism laid down by Aristotle. In the more particular doctrines, which refer to plot, character, and diction, he approaches somewhat nearer to our modern conceptions of realism.

In the question of plot, we must notice those remarks which later became the basis of the dogma of the Three Unities, but which, in Aristotle himself, are loosely and vaguely expressed. There is, in the first place, the Unity of Plot: "...in poetry the story, as an imitation of action, must represent one action, a complete whole, with its several incidents so closely connected that the transposal or withdrawal of any one of them will disjoin and dislocate the whole".[1] The Unity of Plot, in fact, is deduced

[1] Ch. 7.

from the general principle of realism, and demands that the events of the play shall have a necessary or a probable connection one with another.[1]

In the matter of diction, it would appear from the *Poetics* alone that Aristotle favoured the use of a manner of speech removed from that of daily life,[2] but there he does not deal with the subject very fully. In the *Rhetoric*, on the other hand, we find this very interesting passage:

We can now see that a writer must disguise his art and give the impression of speaking naturally and not artificially. Naturalness is persuasive, artificiality is the contrary; for our hearers are prejudiced and think we have some design against them, as if we were mixing their wines for them.... We can hide our purpose successfully by taking the single words of our composition from the speech of ordinary life. This is

[1] *Ibid.* "In writing an *Odyssey* he (Homer) did not make the poem cover all that ever befell his hero—it befell him, for instance, to get wounded on Parnassus and also to feign madness at the time of the call to arms, but the two incidents had no necessary or probable connection with one another—instead of doing so he took an action with a Unity of the kind we describe."

[2] Ch. 22, v, especially the commendation of Euripides for the introduction of θοινᾶται for ἐσθίει in the line of Aeschylus:

Φαγέδαινα ἥ μου σάρκας ἐσθίει ποδός,

done in poetry by Euripides, who was the first to show the way to his successors.[1]

The first sentence here—"the writer must give the impression of speaking naturally and not artificially"—is again a general statement of the demands of realism in diction which we shall hardly be able to make more specific. It will apply equally to poetic drama and to prose drama, for in either case, the dramatist must not make his characters say anything that is not either necessary or probable. And it is worth noting that the diction of Shakespeare's people is not, in *actual effect on the stage*, more unrealistic than the speeches of Shaw or Wilde, or Congreve or Sheridan. If there is a difference between them, it does not lie in this.

In the matter of character, Aristotle's definition of realism is much more specific, and raises questions of much wider interest:

The objects the imitator represents are actions, with agents who are necessarily either good men or bad—the diversities of human character being nearly always derived from this primary distinction, since the line between virtue and vice is one dividing the whole of mankind. It follows, therefore, that the

[1] III, 2, 5.

[11]

agents represented must be either above our level of goodness, or beneath it, or just such as we are; in the same way as, with the painters, the personages of Polygnotus are better than we are, those of Pauson worse, and those of Dionysius just like ourselves.... Homer's personages, for instance, are better than we are; Cleophon's are on our own level; and those of Hegemon of Thasos, the first writer of parodies, and Nicochares, the author of the *Diliad*, are beneath it.[1]

Here obviously, the type of personage "just such as we are" represents realism in character, and is as good a general definition as we may find. But it is significant that, as Aristotle goes on, he points out that the two great divisions of the drama are based on the two extreme types of character, those better, and those worse than ourselves: "This difference it is that distinguishes Tragedy and Comedy also; the one would make its personages worse, and the other better, than the men of the present day".[2]

This passage is, in a sense, the text of our essay on realism in the drama. In it, we find the critical definitions of the two types of drama known to the Greeks, Tragedy and Comedy, and it is apparent that in neither of these two kinds is there

[1] Ch. 2.   [2] *Ibid.*

any scope for the middle type of personage, the realistic character "just like ourselves". We shall see how the notions of these two types of drama, supported by the authority of Aristotle, became more and more a critical dogma, limiting the freedom of expression of the creative artist ever more rigidly, until various efforts were made to find a new form, a type of drama that was neither Tragedy nor Comedy. And it is in these attempts to escape the critical categories of the Greeks that we shall find our nearest approximation to a consistent notion of the realistic drama—the drama whose characters are neither better nor worse than ourselves, but "on our own level".

I would add, in conclusion to this section of our work, that this particular question offers more scope for the application of the point of view which we have chosen than almost any other branch of art. It so happened that the drama was the first subject of the first critic—Aristotle; and it happened further that this critic had an altogether exceptional ability in the framing of just definitions. Through various historical accidents, his authority was revived many centuries after his death, and his categories were applied to art produced in circumstances totally different from those in which he had written. Thus it happens that in the drama, the conflict between criticism and creative expression may be most clearly observed and studied.

II. THE PRACTICE OF GREEK DRAMA

From the historical point of view, the practice of Greek drama is not nearly so important as the theory based upon it by Aristotle. The imitators of the Greeks in the seventeenth century were less concerned with the models than with the principles of the *Poetics*, and in general we may say that the critics were in a stronger position than the creative writers throughout this period. Thus, from our present point of view, the actual works of the Greeks are chiefly important in so far as they throw some light on Aristotle's theories.

We have already referred to the main practical problem which arises here. Aristotle insists that the events of the play shall be either necessarily produced one from another, or of the order of probability which we find in our life from day to day. Yet we see in the works of the tragedians the most improbable events performed or related; gods come upon the scene, and take a part in the action, and we hear of monsters coming out from the sea (in the *Hippolytus*), of women so over-come with madness that they tear to pieces the son of one of their number (in the *Bacchae*), and of ghosts rising from their tombs (in the *Persae*). There is an apparent inconsistency here. But Aristotle himself points the way to its explanation in his statement that Tragedy, in which, naturally, these events are more common than in Comedy, is largely concerned with the past.

This statement deserves more attention than is generally paid to it. In a word, it amounts to this: that almost the whole of the Greek drama (Comedy aside) is what we should call historical drama. The works of Aeschylus, Sophocles, and Euripides which have come down to us are all historical plays.

Too often this has been overlooked, and for two reasons. Firstly, it has been the fashion since the Renaissance to exaggerate the extent to which the Athenians were civilised, and to forget that with them the typical achievements of civilisa-tion, such as abstract thought, logic, and abstract art,[1] were very new discoveries, which had not, in the great epoch of Athenian culture, entirely ousted, but only overlaid the old primitive culture which lay behind them. The recognition of this truth has led to the most valuable results in the study of Greek thought and philosophy,[2] but so far it has not been very generally realised by students of Greek art.

And secondly, we are accustomed to explain the theology and the theological stories of the Greeks as "mythological", whereas we should suppose that to the Greeks themselves, these stories were, in the strictest sense of the word, *history*. One has only to remember the attitude to the stories of the Bible which prevailed until the last century to realise all that this implies. Just as Christians of the old school were profoundly shocked by the Darwinian account of the creation because they felt it to be on the same

[1] I use this term rather loosely here, but mean to indicate the peculiar achievement of the sculpture of the sixth and fifth centuries, which shows, in the sphere of plastic art, the increasing aptitude for abstraction which appeared also in Socrates, and which was an entirely new thing in Europe.

[2] The work of Professor Cornford is particularly important in this connection.

level as the account in Genesis, and to be con-
tradictory to it, so the Greeks would have
been very shocked at any modern account of
the ancient history of their race which did
not adhere strictly to the account given in their
myths.

The Greeks who composed the audience in the
theatre at Athens were, in fact, still to a large extent a primitive people, who took great pleasure,
as all primitive peoples do, in hearing of their
own past, in a form which we should call mythological, but which was strict history, narration of
plain fact, to them.

So we must be prepared to modify to some
extent the general view that the Greek tragedy
was absolutely unrealistic. Taking into account
all the usual considerations—the masks, the
buskins, and scene, the music, and above all the
chorus, still we may say that the effect upon a
Greek audience was much more realistic than it is
to us, and events which we may consider to be
very far removed from the common standard of
human probability, to them seemed natural and
realistic enough. They actually had *happened* at
some time in the past, and the only difference between them and the events of daily life was that

the standard of probability was taken from the past.

Thus we shall do well to add a method of classifying plots which Aristotle did not mention: the events of the drama may be represented as happening in the past, in the present, or in the future. For events must happen in time, and events in time must fall in one or other of these three divisions. Plots of events in the past are obviously realistic in the sense that they describe real events, things which have actually happened; but, in general, the standard of probability in such plots is also taken from the past, and is not necessarily the same as that of the present. We shall consider this question more fully in relation to the historical play proper.

Plots of events represented in the future are generally the least realistic. I cannot recall any examples in antiquity, but in the modern drama an obvious example would be Capek's *R.U.R.*

And of course plots representing events as taking place in the present are the most realistic.

We may add a similar classification based on the relation of the plot to space. Plots represented as taking place far away may attain to the same kind of realism as the plot in the past; they

may represent things which are supposed to have
happened in fact, but which are to be judged by a
different standard of probability from that of
the everyday life of the audience. In the Greek
drama, this type of plot is not of much importance, naturally enough, for the Greeks did not
know of lands very far distant from their own;
though we may cite the *Persae* as an example
among surviving plays. It would hardly have
been possible to represent the ghost of a nearly
contemporary Athenian on the stage; distance in
this case lends the same liberties as lapse of time.[1]

Plots may be represented as happening off the
earth altogether, as in the *Clouds* of Aristophanes,
and this, like the plot in the future, tends to be the
least realistic.

And finally, plots may be represented as taking
place *here* and *now*, in the same place as the
audience, and in the present. It is under these circumstances that the greatest effect of realism is
attained. And an obvious example in Greece is the
work of Aristophanes which, for the most part,

[1] This is particularly important in the Elizabethan
drama. Most of the plots of the Elizabethans are represented as taking place in some foreign country, generally
vaguely Italian.

takes plots referring to contemporary Athenian history, and is entirely realistic in treatment.

This leads us to our final consideration on the practice of the Greeks, that comedy was naturally much nearer to our conceptions of realism than tragedy, and, as we shall see, the achievement of realism in the drama may, from one point of view, be regarded as the importation of comic methods into the matter and atmosphere of tragedy.

A further examination of the case of comedy may more properly be reserved for the next chapter, in which we shall deal with Roman drama. For the Roman comedy happens to have survived the fortunes of time better than the Greek, and the later history of the drama owes much more to Plautus and to Terence than to Aristophanes.

For the moment, we may notice that the practice of the Greeks raises the most important questions which bear upon our subject—the exact place of the historical drama, the relation of the plot to time and place, and the relative realism of comedy as compared with tragedy. We are not attempting a full examination of Greek drama, and we may be content to leave it, now that we have passed from it to these more general questions.

CHAPTER III

ROME: COMEDY

I. THEORY

THE theory of the drama was not developed in Roman criticism much beyond the point reached by Aristotle, and in the matter of tragedy, at any rate, its historical importance was not very great.[1] The *Ars Poetica* of Horace has many lesser virtues, which make it more readable than works which are, in content, much more important, but it can hardly be maintained that it added anything very original to dramatic theory. From our present point of view, almost the only passage to which we should call attention is that on verisimilitude:

Ficta voluptatis causa sint proxima veris,
Ne quodcunque velit poscat sibi fabula credi,
Neu pransae Lamiae vivum puerum extrahat alvo.[2]

A very reasonable warning, but one which hardly adds to the view of the question which we have already found in Aristotle.

[1] I have reached this conclusion after a full consideration of the fact that the influence of Horace was felt in the Renaissance very much earlier than that of Aristotle.
[2] Ll. 338–340.

In the theory of comedy, however, the situation is different, largely owing to the accident which has deprived us of the second part of the *Poetics* of Aristotle—the part which seems to have dealt with comedy. Thus it happened that the Roman theory of comedy was the only theory available in the Renaissance, and its importance was considerable. It is perhaps unfortunate, from the point of view of the critic, that this theory happens to be expressed in such an awkward form—in the form, that is, of *scholia* on the plays of Terence written mainly by the grammarian Donatus. However, we must try to extract from these notes the general outline of the theory of comedy which certainly formed the basis of the Renaissance theory, and practice.

The most consecutive piece of Donatus is a fragment to which the heading "De Comoedia et Tragedia" has been affixed.[1] It is in this fragment that we find the notion, which later formed the basis of the theory of comedy, that comedy is the "mirror of human life". According to

[1] This is published very conveniently with the text of Terence, with many other critical selections on him, and complete scholia in the Delphinium edition of 1675, but is available, of course, in any other standard edition.

[22]

Donatus, this was first expressed by Livius
Andronicus:

Comoediam esse quotidianae vitae speculum.

Whether Livius originated this view or not, it is
remarkably like a general view of realistic drama.
In particular, it should be noticed that the phrase
contains the essential adjective "quotidiana",[1]
which brings it nearer to explicit realistic principles than any other similar phrase in ancient
criticism. This aspect is well developed by
Donatus, who makes it the chief difference between comedy and tragedy; comedy, he says,
deals with the fortunes of private persons, whose
lives are composed of mediocre events, while
tragedy takes place "in aulis regiis", in the halls
of kings, whose lives contain the very greatest
and most impressive happenings.

Throughout the scholia on the text, Donatus

[1] A consideration not raised in the longer quotation
from Cicero, which is generally given as the source of this
theory (e.g. by Professor Saintsbury, who does not seem
to have been quite accurate on the whole question). It
should be noted, perhaps, that a very similar phrase occurs
in Terence himself: "denique
Inspicere tanquam in speculum, in vitas omnium
Jubeo, atque ex aliis sumere exemplum sibi"

(*Adelphi*, III, iii, 60–62).

adheres to, and expands this theory, and adds to it a steady insistence on the difference between tragedy and comedy in minor respects—in diction, and in the amount and quality of the sympathy excited in the audience.[1]

Thus, in spite of the form in which they were expressed, the theories of Donatus lay down certain principles which are of the utmost importance for the later history of the drama. In him we find the first clear expression of the view that comedy is realistic, dealing with the lives of ordinary people, and attempting to reproduce them with the fidelity of a mirror; and—perhaps even more important—he gives expression to the rigid distinction between tragedy and comedy. We shall find that both of these things have important consequences.

II. THE PRACTICE OF ROMAN DRAMA

In the practice of the Roman drama we must distinguish two tendencies, one of which supports the principle of realism as laid down by Donatus, and another which, potentially at any rate, conflicts with it, and which in the Renaissance did a

[1] E.g. scholia to *Adel.* IV, iv, 4; to *Phormio Prol.* 5, 6, 8, and 1, i, 7, ii, 33, 41, 45, 87, etc.

good deal to hinder the development of true
realism.

The realistic aspect of Roman comedy is obvious enough, and we need not stress it at great
length; the diction of both Terence and of
Plautus, but especially of Plautus, is evidently
much nearer to the spoken language than anything else in ancient drama, with a vocabulary
which almost becomes slang, and an order of
words which is very different from that usually
found in Latin verse, and apparently much nearer
to the order of common speech. The characters
are taken from the middle classes and from those
connected with them, so that the people on the
stage would be very like the majority of people
in the audience. And the plots were composed of
events which might well occur in the lives of the
audience themselves—spendthrift sons, rascally
slaves, women and wine, demands on the father's
purse.

So far, the Roman comedy was evidently far
on the path towards realism. But simultaneously
it was developing a tendency which conflicts very
strongly with realism—the tendency which I
shall describe, I hope clearly, as the *stylisation of
character*. Briefly, this consists in adopting a rigid

model for the character of various persons—the son, the slave, the father, the courtesan, and so forth—and in conforming their actions and their speech exactly to this model in such a way that they are not represented as individual beings at all. This is connected, of course, with the practice of naming characters by means of adaptations of the names of qualities which distinguish them. Donatus gives several examples of this in a scholium: "Nomina personarum, in comoediis duntaxat, habere debent rationem & etymologiam....Hinc servus fidelis *Parmeno*: infidelis vel *Syrus*, vel *Geta*: miles *Thraso*, vel *Polemon*: juvenis *Pamphilus*: matrona *Myrrhina*...."[1]

This leads to a type of character very far from realistic, a personage who is not a human being in any sense, but a mere *dramatised personification*. And it was a development of this practice in theory which led Rymer, as we shall see, to one of the most anti-realistic theories of the drama ever propounded. The practice itself we find again in the Restoration drama, where it does much to exclude from the category of realism a type of play which might otherwise have fallen within it.

[1] Scholium to *Adelphi*, i, i, i.

But in spite of this tendency to stylisation of the characters, we may conclude that, on the whole, the Roman comedy set a model of realism which was of great importance after the Renaissance, and which entirely justifies the theory of the "mirror of life" based upon it by Donatus.

Here we may conclude our account of the ancient theory and practice of the drama. For the most part, it does not exhibit fully the conflict of critics and creative writers, because both Aristotle and Donatus wrote after the great creative periods, and based their theories upon the spontaneously produced forms of the dramatists. It is later, after the Renaissance, that the conflict develops, when the theories of Aristotle and of Donatus were applied to a living tradition of drama, curtailing its freedom, and in some ways creating the most serious difficulties for the artist. But before we come to this conflict, we must deal with another period of free, uncritical creation—that of the Elizabethans.

Note

In passing from the Roman drama to the Elizabethans, it is obvious that we are neglecting a fairly large body of material belonging to the Middle Ages. And if we were attempting a history of the drama, this would be inexcusable. But we are not attempting such a history, and the omission is sufficiently justified by the fact that very little can be discovered about realism in this field that cannot be seen more clearly in more familiar work. It is enough to remark that what we have said of the Greek drama is generally true of the mediaeval—it is essentially a historical drama, and all that we could say about it from our point of view we shall say about historical drama in general.

CHAPTER IV

THE ELIZABETHAN DRAMA

I. THEORY

THE theory of the Elizabethan drama need hardly detain us at all. For most practical purposes, it had little effect on the creative work of the period, excepting in a few plays of Ben Jonson, and those his least successful.

The chief document of the theory is, of course, Sidney's "Apologie for Poetrie". Here two things are to be noticed. First, the insistence on the importance of the Unities as a means to realism, and secondly the censure of tragi-comedy. Sidney gives a spirited description of the demands made on the imagination by the average play of his time:

...you shal have Asia of the one side, and Affrick of the other, and so many other under-kingdoms, that the Player, when he commeth in, must ever begin with telling where he is: or els the tale wil not be conceived? Now ye shal have three Ladies walke to gather flowers, and then we must beleeve the stage to be a garden. By and by we heare newes of shipwracke in the same place, and then wee are to blame if we accept it not for a Rock. Upon the backe of that, comes out a hidious monster, with fire and smoke, and then the miserable beholders are bounde to take it for a Cave. While in the meantime two Armies flye in, represented with foure swords and bucklers, and then what harde heart will not receive it for a pitched fielde? Now of time they are much more liberall, for ordinary it is that two young Princes fall in love. After many traverces, she is got with childe, delivered of a faire boy; he is lost, groweth a man, falls in love, and is ready to get another childe; and all this in two hours space.[1]

Here we find implicit the common assumptions of those who upheld the theory of the Unities. Fundamentally, they believed that the most satisfactory dramatic illusion—the greatest realism—is attainable only by recognising the limitations of stage presentation. The stage is one place in fact: and so the drama must conform with the Unity of Place. The time of the presentation is limited: and the time of the plot must therefore be limited, must conform with the Unity of Time. We shall see later that this is wrong simply because it is not an adequate description of the real situation in the theatre; it leaves out of account the psychological attitude and expectations of

[1] I quote from the text given in Mr Brimley Johnson's *Poetry and the Poets*.

the audience. Sidney concludes strongly for the Unities, and his pronouncement is interesting as being the first in English: "...the stage should alwaies represent but one place, and the uttermost time presupposed in it should be, both by Aristotle's precept and common reason, but one day...". Fortunately for us, the dramatists paid little attention to this, and achieved their realism by other means.

Sidney also complains of tragi-comedy:

> But besides these grosse absurdities, how all theyr Playes be neither right Comedies nor right Tragedies, mingling Kings and Clownes, not because the matter so carrieth it, but thrust in Clownes by head and shoulders, to play a part in maiesticall matters, with neither decencie nor discretion, so as neither the admiration and commiseration, nor the right sportfulness, is by their mungrell Tragy-comedie obtained.

Here is a typical case of the rigid definition of the forms of art by criticism. Drama must be either tragic or comic, it must obey the very definite rules set down for each kind,[1] and no other form of dramatic expression is possible or allowable. We can only consider it fortunate that the genius of the Elizabethans was uncritical, and that the

[1] *V.* for example Scaliger, *Poetices Libri,* vi.

[31]

dramatists were, above all, practical writers, most of them working in very close contact with the stage itself and with the actors, so that the rules which they followed were, like the rules followed in Greek drama, derived from the material conditions of the stage and its arrangement. In the Greek drama, the chorus, which is on the stage during the whole of the presentation, makes adherence to the Unities of Place and Time a necessity. In the Elizabethan drama, all characters have "their exits and their entrances", and so the continuity of the place and the time, which, as Corneille very rightly pointed out,[1] are affixed to the characters, and not to the scene, may easily be broken.

It should be noticed that Sidney gives no theoretical defence of the definition of drama as either tragic or comic. It does not rest on any assumptions concerning the nature of dramatic illusion, as the theory of the Unities does. And as far as I can discover, the matter is not more fully explained in the Italian critics upon whom Sidney based his views. Yet it would be a mis-

[1] *Discours des Trois Unités*, particularly the theory of "le lieu théatral", which plainly attaches the place to the characters.

take, I think, to regard it as a mere dogma. For, although its supporters never give this reason in its favour, it clearly depends on the important consideration that the audience have certain expectations and preconceptions of the drama, and that any serious failure to fulfil these expectations, any large divergence from the preconceived notion of a drama, will result in a loss of verisimilitude. In actual practice, of course, this does not serve to support the attack on tragi-comedy; it only held good for that minority of the Elizabethan (or Italian) audience which was well acquainted with the ancient drama. The greater part of the audience would have more general preconceptions, which would find no difficulty at all in accommodating tragi-comedy. But in general theory, we must recognise that the preconceptions of the audience must be taken into consideration as a factor in the production of a realistic effect. We shall return to this subject later.

Apart from Sidney, we need not consider in detail any Elizabethan critics. The few remarks of Ben Jonson on the drama add nothing to the view of the Unities found in Sidney, and certainly add nothing more to the general theory of realism. Perhaps we should mention the well-known passage from Hamlet, where Shakespeare explains, apparently, his own theory of the drama:

...for anything so overdone is from the purpose of playing, whose end, both at the first and now, was and is, to hold, as 'twere, the mirror up to nature; to show virtue her own feature, scorn her own image, and the very age and body of the time his form and pressure....[1]

Apart from the fact that we have the old image of the "mirror of nature" here, the passage would seem rather to be a condemnation of "over-acting" than a definite expression of dramatic theory. And, in any case, it adds little to what we already know. From Shakespeare's practice, on the other hand, we may learn a great deal; and to this we shall now pass.

II. ELIZABETHAN PRACTICE

(a) Tragi-comedy

The form of tragi-comedy has been attacked generally on grounds of pure critical theory, and the condemnation of it which we have already quoted from Sidney may stand as typical of

[1] Act III, sc. 2.

almost all other condemnations. But the argu-
ments which have been urged in its defence are
more various. The most general is to be found in
Dryden's *Essay on Dramatick Poesy*, and we must
so far anticipate the historical order of our expo-
sition as to quote from it:

He (Lisideius) tells us, we cannot so speedily
recollect ourselves after a scene of great passion and
concernment, as to pass to another of mirth and
humour, and to enjoy it with any relish: but why
should he imagine the soul of man more heavy than
his senses? Does not the eye pass from an unpleasant
object to a pleasant in a much shorter time than is
required to this? and does not the unpleasantness of
the first commend the beauty of the latter? The old
rule of logick might have convinced him, that con-
traries, when placed near, set off each other. A continued gravity keeps the spirit too much bent; we
must refresh it sometimes, as we bait in a journey,
that we may go on with greater ease. A scene of
mirth, mixed with tragedy, has the same effect upon
us which our musick has between the acts; which we
find a relief to us from the best plots and language of
the stage...we have invented, increased, and per-
fected a more pleasant way of writing for the stage,
than was ever known to the ancients or moderns of
any nation, which is tragi-comedy.[1]

[1] From the speech of Neander.

The general argument here is in accordance with the hedonistic principles of Dryden's theory of art. The comic relief is not regarded as anything more than a variation, a pause, as it were, in the real business, during which the audience may sit back in their seats and gather strength for the more serious parts of the play.

Coleridge has a most interesting passage on the same subject, which shows certain affinities with that of Dryden, but which also introduces other considerations, and particularly refers to our problem of realism:

> Shakespeare found the infant stage demanding an intermixture of ludicrous character as imperiously as that of Greece did the chorus, and high language accordant. And there are many advantages in this;— a greater assimilation to nature, a greater scope of power, more truths and more feelings;—the effects of contrast, as in Lear and the Fool....[1]

This notion of contrast, which we have seen too in the Dryden passage above, Coleridge attributes to Plato:

> In another passage he even adds the reason (*sc.* why the tragic poet should also be able to write comedy), namely, that opposites illustrate each other's nature,

[1] Lecture on the Progress of the Drama.

and in their struggle draw forth the strength of the combatants, and display the conqueror as sovereign even on the territories of the rival power.[1]

While admitting that these are all very good reasons for the use of tragi-comedy made by Shakespeare, we may add another consideration from our present point of view, that the mixture of the comic with the tragic contributes very largely to the realistic effect.[2] Let us examine this in detail.

In the first place, it should be noticed that comedy, portraying characters "worse than ourselves", is more realistic in the nature of things than tragedy, which portrays people better than ourselves. This is explicable in many ways: perhaps good men are not so common as bad men— that is the simplest explanation. Or it may be that pride leads us to consider few better than ourselves, and many worse. In any case, the ideals of

[1] Lecture on the Greek Drama. He refers, of course, to the *Ion*.

[2] I am not sure whether Coleridge means the same by his phrase "a greater assimilation to nature". Possibly he does, but it seems more likely that he wished to say that since life itself is composed of the comic and the tragic together, a drama which includes both will be more lifelike than one which does not. This is not what I wish to say.

[37]

character are, for the very reason that they are ideals, rarely if ever realised, while it is always easy enough to find men who are very far below the ideal standards. Thus, one way or another, the number of men worse than ourselves, in our own estimation, will always be greater than the number of those better than ourselves, in our own estimation. And, since it is natural enough to consider the kind of man which we find most common to be the most real, it comes about that comedy is more real than tragedy. This, as we have seen, is reflected in the ancient theory of comedy as the "mirror of nature".

A further consideration is this, that in all society moral standards of value tend to become confused with social standards. In his definitions, Aristotle does not clearly specify the respect in which the characters of comedy are worse than ourselves, and though we may assume that he meant in respect of morality, it is easy enough to believe that he too had some notion of the social scale. Certainly in spite of his attempt to assign a definite kind of inferiority in the terms of his definition,[1] the critics who followed him made the difference a purely social one. Thus Scaliger:

[1] *Poetics*, 5.

THE ELIZABETHAN DRAMA

"In illa (comoedia) e pagis sumpti Chremetes, Davi, Thaides, loco humili:.... In Tragoedia Reges, Principes...".[1] And since the lower classes are more numerous than the upper classes —οἱ πολλοί, "the many-headed", the same argument holds as in the general case of people worse than ourselves: because there are more of them, we think of them as more real.

This consideration is of the greatest importance in the later history of realism, and we shall return to it. But we have said enough here to make Shakespeare's use of it understandable.

It is obvious enough that Shakespeare does use the lower classes in this way, from the fact that he is accustomed to make them speak in prose, while characters of higher social station speak in verse.[2] This may be observed in a great number of passages—for the sake of an example, in the opening scene of *Julius Caesar*, where Flavius and Marullus, the tribunes, speak in verse, while "certain Commoners" speak in prose; and similarly in the opening scene of Coriolanus.

[1] *Loc. cit.*
[2] Let us take this for granted at the moment—as, I think, Shakespeare took it for granted. It became a question of theoretical discussion only in the Restoration, and we shall deal with it when we come to that period.

[39]

In particular plays, Shakespeare uses this in effect (intended or not) as a device for introducing realism and maintaining the dramatic illusion. Most cleverly, perhaps, in the *Tempest*, where the supernatural personage of Caliban is brought into the closest connection with those characters of the play who have the most realistic flavour about them—Stephano and Trinculo. So successful is this device, that the average audience finds no difficulty in giving full credence to the character of Caliban, and indeed hardly notices that he is not a human character at all. Notice too that their conversation together is carried on in prose.

In the historical plays something of the same kind is used to add to the effect of battle scenes, always the parts of the play which put the greatest strain on the willingness of the audience to be deceived. The most notable examples are the two battles in the two parts of *King Henry IV*, at which Falstaff makes his appearances as a warrior. The more closely one examines these scenes, the more one must admire the way in which the fat knight, without diminishing the suspense, the motion, and the excitement by the laughter which he must provoke, serves to add to the realism of the scenes, and to make them the most credible battles of the Elizabethan stage.¹ So well did it serve his purpose, that Shakespeare repeats the same device in the battle in *King Henry the Fifth*, with the poor relics of the Falstaffian world, Nym, Pistol, Bardolph, and the Boy, who delivers in the midst of the battle a long comic prose soliloquy exactly in the manner of his late master, and where Pistol achieves a faint imitation of the capture of Colevile on the person of a French soldier.²

Finally, we may notice the use of the Fool in *Lear* which Coleridge was never tired of commending. The Fool not only serves "to heighten and inflame the passion of the scene"³ on the heath; he also serves to lend it a realism which it is famed for possessing, and which it

---

¹ A very similar device is used in Calderon's *Life's a Dream*, where the clown of the play, Clarin, hides behind a rock during the battle, first adding to the effect by his realistic comments, and then himself dying from a stray arrow. I know of few more affecting things in the drama than this death of the clown (cf. *Lear*, where, however, we do not see the Fool die). The mere fact that he is the clown, and so in a sense more real than the other characters, makes his death more moving, and the death by a *stray* arrow enormously enhances the effect of the battle. ² Act IV, sc. 4. ³ *Notes on Lear*.

might not otherwise possess, at any rate in the same degree, if he, with his comic and realistic associations, and his prose, were absent from it.

We need hardly carry our analysis of Shakespeare's use of tragi-comedy further. I do not say that it was only for this reason that he used it, or even that he was conscious of using it for this reason, but it should be clear that in effect it leads to some of his most realistic scenes. The device was simple, depending on nothing more than the fact that the traditional associations of comedy are with realism, and that its method—prose—and its characters—worse than ourselves—both contribute to the same end.

Shakespeare's practice is the final answer to any theoretical condemnation of tragi-comedy, the final justification of the freedom of creative expression, as opposed to the definitions of critics. And we may notice here that the form of tragi-comedy is the first form of realistic drama, paving the way for the drama of personages "just like ourselves" by the abolition of the categories of Tragedy and Comedy, which will include only characters worse, or better, than ourselves.[1]

[1] *V.* p. 13.

(b) The Historical Drama

Although I have endeavoured to show that the Greek drama must be considered in the category of historical drama, I have deferred consideration of the subject until this point, because the appropriate problems are more conveniently seen in connection with that drama which is based on our own history; and by this I mean the histories of Shakespeare, together with the *Edward the Second* of Marlowe. As Coleridge says: "In order that a drama may be properly historical, it is necessary that it should be the history of the people to whom it is addressed".[1]

We may well agree that this remark is true, but we must regret that Coleridge did not think it necessary to adduce any reasons for its truth—for it is a difficult matter to supply them. Partly, no doubt, it is because any audience is naturally more interested in the events of the history of their own nation, which give rise to a more interesting concernment in the fortunes of war, and in the general glory of their past. This appeal

[1] *Note on Shakespeare's English Historical Plays.*

to patriotism is found already in *King Richard the Second*, in John of Gaunt's famous speech, which must be placed with Virgil's praise of Italy as the greatest expression of patriotic feeling in poetry; and it is continued through the battles of the later reigns.

"Patriotism": it is a vague enough word at the best, and I am not much inclined to use it freely in criticism without any attempt at analysis. Especially since, in one of its aspects at least, it would seem to be of great importance from the point of view of culture and art. For, apart from its more obvious implications, such as love of one's own country, a desire to serve it, to fight for it, to respect its institutions, and prefer them to the institutions of all other countries—apart from all these meanings, patriotism is the embodiment and expression of the feeling of national historical continuity in the majority of the race. What, in a philosopher or a critic, we should call "the historical sense", in an ordinary man we call (or should call) patriotism; at all events, the notion of patriotism is hardly conceivable without some knowledge of the history of the nation, and it is certain that this knowledge, even in forms which might be called mythological, penetrates into places where other parts of education have never found an entrance.

The most important consequence of this feeling of continuity is the concernment which is begotten by wars of the past. Any child, and—though this is not so praiseworthy—many adult historians "take sides" in the affairs of the past, are Saxons or Normans, Red Roses or White Roses, Cavaliers or Roundheads. And this, to a large extent, depends on the feeling of continuity, the intimate causal connection of all the events which make up our history: if things had not turned out then as we want them, or as we would have wanted them, then things now would not be as they are, would be somehow quite different, and we ourselves might not even exist. Thus, in a sense, our own existence is guaranteed by history, and, conversely, our own existence guarantees the truth of history, because both belong to the same causal chain of events.

It is easy to see that this is of the greatest importance in the historical drama. The actions represented on the stage so intimately concern every person present that, if they do not turn out in the right way for him, he will meet with an almost personal disaster—his very existence will be endangered, as a social, national being. As a matter of fact, of course, things always do turn out as he would have them, for the historical drama never represents the reverses which a nation has suffered,[1] and always its successes—or if it does deal with what history calls a reverse, it takes the liberty of representing it as a success. Thus it comes about that in the historical drama there is a most intimate connection between the events on the stage and the audience. The events on the stage, in fact, are the *cause* of the audience: "It is because these things have happened so that we now can sit here and enjoy in security the advantages of our national theatre. Had the French conquered us, there might never have been a theatre at all, and this entertainment would never have taken place".

All this follows from the appreciation of the causal connection of national history. I do not say that it follows consciously—quite the opposite; but it is, I think, included in the notion of

---

[1] One remembers the unfortunate Athenian dramatist who was heavily fined for representing the defeat of Athens at sea during the war with Sparta.

patriotism, especially when we consider the kind
of historical patriotism involved in the "taking
sides" over affairs in the past.[1] And obviously
it means that the historical drama possesses a
peculiar kind of realism all of its own. Through
this feeling of patriotism, national continuity, the
events on the stage confirm the existence of the
audience, and conversely, the existence of the
audience confirms the truth of the events on the
stage. In no other type of drama is such a remarkable connection formed between the play
and the audience, and this alone makes the
historical play always realistic.

Always realistic even when certain events con-
tradict the common laws of human probability,
as long as such events have the authority of history or myth. This was pointed out by Aristotle
in connection with the Greek drama, and holds
good of all historical drama. And Coleridge

[1] I should like, by the way, to draw attention to the way
in which every man tends, with the Athenians, to take
great pride in being *indigenous*. Thus children with the
strongest Norman or Celtic racial characteristics will un-
hesitatingly side with the Saxons against the Normans,
or against the Celts. Whatever history may say, we all
feel that our stock is the real English, and has inhabited
the place where we now live from the beginning of
history.

[47]

uses the same principle in connection with
Lear:[1]

It may be worthy of notice that Lear is the only
serious performance of Shakspeare, the interest and
situation of which are derived from the assumption of
a gross improbability;...but observe the matchless
judgement of our Shakspeare. First, improbable as
the conduct of Lear is in the first scene, yet it was an
old story rooted in the popular faith,—a thing taken
for granted already, and consequently without any
effects of improbability.[2]

---

[1] At first sight, Coleridge's inclusion of *Lear* among
the historical plays may seem a little strange. But on
reflection, it will be seen to be just. Lear was an English
king, and, for the audience who had never been taught to
regard part of history as mythological, that was enough.
The kind of historical knowledge which is a part of
patriotism is precisely the kind which would regard Lear
as true history, on a par with the history of Henry IV, or
any other English king, just as the Greeks, in a similar
position, and with a similar degree of popular education,
would regard their own myths as true history. We need
not make any distinction, in fact, between a historical
play, and a "historico-mythological" play. We have only
to put ourselves in the position of an audience of that age
—Elizabethan or Athenian—to see that they are the same
thing.

[2] *Notes on Lear*. Elsewhere, Coleridge does not adhere to the same principle: "In the composition, care
must be taken that there appear no dramatic improbability,
as the reality is taken for granted" (*Note on Shakespeare's*

To this main consideration of the realism of
the historical drama, we may add the minor consideration that its plot is geographically near to
us. In Shakespeare's plays, for example, many
scenes take place in London, in the place of the
representation, and it cannot be denied that this
adds considerably to the effect of realism.[1]

There is, however, one respect in which the
historical play differs from the ordinary realistic
play. Its characters are, for the most part, socially
better than ourselves. The chronicles of time are
chronicles of Kings, not of merchants or clerks,
and only the great actions are remembered. Pri-

English Historical Plays). But the other passage expresses
a truer view. The inconsistency, however, serves to
show that Coleridge had not penetrated very deeply into
the problem.

[1] An obvious comparison from the Greek drama
suggests itself: the last scene of the *Oresteia*, where Orestes
comes for judgment to the court of Athens. According to
some authorities, this had a definitely political purpose,
and was intended to support the reforms of Pericles in the
judicial system carried out in the year before the production of the play. This court was reduced from being a sort
of House of Lords, to a purely judicial court in cases of
homicide. This well illustrates the historical nature of the
Greek drama; no one would adduce a myth in support of
a political reform, but anyone would adduce a *historical
precedent* for the purpose.

vate persons, and private actions, which compose
the ordinary realistic drama, are forgotten, or
never known outside the family.

And for this reason, as well as for the fact that
the particular kind of realistic illusion which it
achieves is peculiar to itself, we must regard the
historical play not as a species of realistic drama,
but as a class apart. Yet we must remember that
it is in practice intensely realistic, and that a large
part of the greatest drama in the world owes its
realism to the fact that it is historical. It should
be noted too that the exponents of the realistic
drama in the nineteenth century (which one
naturally regards as the most typical realistic
drama) often confused ordinary realism and
historical realism. Both Ibsen and Strindberg
wrote historical plays, and with both the writing
of them was of the greatest importance from a
technical point of view. In the realistic novel,
the same thing is observed; Flaubert, after
writing *Madame Bovary*, turned to historical
realism in *Salammbô*. And in our own period,
Bernard Shaw has turned from the modern
realistic drama to the historical realism of *Saint
Joan*.

Thus, it is clear that realism is intimately connected with the historical in literature. I hope I have done something to show that this is so, in what respects the two resemble one another, and in what they differ.

(c) The Domestic Drama

The domestic drama is a simpler matter altogether. Here we have certainly a more obvious kind of realism than any we have yet met with, and we need only concern ourselves with the exact means by which it is attained. Its most obvious exponent is, of course, Heywood,[1] but it may be questioned whether any work of his equals *Arden of Feversham*,[2] which seems to me to be superior to any other domestic play of the period, in England at any rate.[3]

[1] Thomas Heywood, of course, not his predecessor John, who hardly merits separate consideration.

[2] The authorship of this play is, certainly, one of the most interesting questions in the sphere of Elizabethan criticism. I can only say that I agree to a non-Shakespearian authorship, and that the attribution to Kyd does not altogether satisfy me.

[3] The qualification is necessary because the contemporary Spanish dramatists produced some admirable domestic drama. In particular, the *Mayor of Zalamea* of Calderon seems to be much superior to *Arden*, or any other play of ours.

In general, the personages of the domestic play are in all respects as like the average member of the audience as they could be. In social station, they are generally of the middle class, not of low birth, like Shakespeare's realistic characters, nor in the rank of tragic events, Kings and Princes.

The scene is laid in England, and very often in London itself, the place of its first presentation.

The period is generally contemporary, although there is often a significant variation towards the type of historical play; for example, in such borderline cases as *The Life of Sir John Oldcastle*,[1] *The Life and Death of the Lord Cromwell*, and *Sir Thomas More*. All these have many scenes which come near the domestic drama, and yet all involve personages of consequence and high place, and are based on history.

For that matter, *Arden* is based on an actual event which, although it took place some forty years before the writing of the play, was apparently still widely known.[2] In cases of this

[1] This play seems to have been written to compete with Shakespeare's Falstaff. It is interesting to compare the two, and only space prevents me from making a detailed comparison.

[2] *Vide* Introduction in the edition of Professor Tucker Brooke, *The Shakespeare Apocrypha*.

kind,[1] where a domestic drama is based upon
some real domestic tragedy, which has stirred
the imagination of a public not yet accustomed
to the evening paper, it is difficult to say where
history ends and fact begins. It is doubtful
whether any dramatist dispenses entirely with
such material—indeed, if we press the question
far enough, it must be allowed that every artist
must take his materials from life, at however
many removes. And it is certain that many have
used real life fairly closely; Ibsen, we may remember, was accustomed in Italy to spend much
of his time in a café, hidden behind a newspaper,
and watching the people around him in a mirror.

But whatever the attitude of the artist to the
events upon which his story is founded, the
Elizabethan audience at least was pleased to find
prefixed to its tragedy the words "The Lament-
able and True Tragedy of...". And in these
circumstances, the effect of realism natural to the
drama of characters just like ourselves was en-
hanced by some of the effects peculiar to the

[1] Webster and Ford, for example, wrote together a
play on *A late Murther of the Sonne upon the Mother*. This
must have been a masterpiece of horror, and we may
regret its loss more than that of its companions of the
same genre.

historical drama. Again we notice the relation between realistic and historical drama.

In all these ways, then, the Elizabethan domestic drama may be called realistic. Judged by any standards extracted from theory or practice prior to it, or contemporary with it, it approximates more obviously to ordinary life than any other type of drama. More obviously, but it may be doubted whether we might add more closely. For if we compare the work of Heywood, or *Arden*, with the plays of the professedly realistic dramatists of the nineteenth century, it is apparent that the approximation to life in the second is closer than it is in the first. What are the reasons for this? Several might be put forward, and some of them at least involve questions of great general importance.

In the first place, it is very possible that the lapse of time may have affected our reaction to the Elizabethan drama considerably. We have spoken already about the significance of the preconceptions of the audience, and the way in which they may affect their attitude to the play. Obviously in the case of all Elizabethan drama, our preconceptions are not "natural", in the sense that our preconceptions about the modern

[54]

drama are natural. They are, necessarily, recon-
structed more or less carefully in normal education, or by irregular, but none the less powerful
means. It is certain, at any rate, that every
member of a modern audience has, in varying
degrees, possessed himself of a general notion of
"the Elizabethan drama", and what it ought to
be. And only too often, this notion is based
almost exclusively upon Shakespeare. This is to
be regretted from a number of points of view,
and not least from that of the Shakespearian himself, who inevitably fails to grasp some aspects of
the poet's greatness through his ignorance of the
more general aspects of the Elizabethan drama.

It is quite certain, at any rate, that among the
Elizabethans themselves, Shakespeare did not
occupy such a prominent position; he was only
one writer among many, and, except in the
opinion of a minority, not very much superior to
the general run of playwrights. Thus their preconception of the drama was likely to be very
different from our own, and with all the will in
the world, we cannot be sure that, by the most
diligent scholarship, we have recaptured a sem-
blance of that preconception. And so it is most
difficult to decide the degree in which the

domestic drama would appear to the contemporary audience as "realistic", in any sense in which Shakespeare was not realistic. It cannot be too much emphasised that analysis according to the objective standards which we have been using—which we are compelled to use, for want of others—such as the social status of the characters, on Aristotelian lines, can only lead to very tentative conclusions. Much more important than any standards of this kind is the contemporary preconception of the drama, and the results which we arrive at without any clear notion of this preconception are most untrustworthy.

Consider, for example, the way in which Heywood introduces sub-plots: his Clowns: his servants,[1] who remind one so much of the Shakespearian low-life characters. It is hardly conceivable that his plays created an effect very different from that of the more normal type of Elizabethan drama, or that they seemed much more realistic to his audience. Yet it is equally hard to believe that his hearer would be entirely insensitive to the fact that the characters were not kings and princes, but common people, like themselves, and that the scene was not in remote

[1] E.g. Jenkin and Cicely in *A Woman Killed with Kindness*.

places, but in England, and that the period was entirely contemporary, and not in some historical or mythological past. It is almost impossible to estimate the force of these opposing considerations: and so impossible to judge accurately the extent of the realistic effect on the contemporary audience.

So much for them; but what of ourselves? Here we are in a position to estimate more nearly the preconception involved, and to estimate its effect on the realism of the domestic play. In the first place, our preconception of Elizabethan drama, being based largely on Shakespeare, gives a very prominent place to the idea of poetry. And at the same time, our preconception of the modern realistic drama includes with equal certainty the notion of prose, as a nearer approximation to the speech of everyday life, and as the practice of the dramatists of the realistic school. How, then, can we feel that Elizabethan drama is realistic, considering that even the writers of the domestic drama employ the form of verse, interspersed with prose to about the same extent as Shakespeare?

There can be no doubt, I think, that the casual reader or the casual audience must find that the employment of a verse form detracts from the realistic effect, even when, as in the greater part of Heywood and of *Arden*, the verse form is completely divorced from poetry. The rhythm of the lines, and the contrast with the prose portions, is enough to remind them of Shakespeare, and so of poetry, the opposite of their notion of realism.

But this consideration does more than explain why most of us find the Elizabethan domestic play comparatively unrealistic: it introduces a matter of the widest general importance for the whole question—how far is realism compatible with poetry? With poetry, that is, not considered as words in the form of verse, as heightened diction, and elevated feeling, but essentially as an attitude to life, a comment on life which is opposed to the comments provided by science, philosophy, or any abstract system of judgments.[1] Poetry, briefly, we shall consider as the imaginative ordering of experience, as opposed to any form of rational ordering.

[1] It becomes apparent here that we cannot avoid the necessity of holding some view on the general questions of aesthetics. For the moment, reference to Coleridge's *Lecture on Shakespeare* with a *Definition of Poetry* will make clear anything that is obscure in the text.

[58]

In general, poetry, of this kind, may take two forms of expression, *myth*, and *metaphor* or *image*. For the moment, I must be excused for this use of dogma: and the meaning may become clearer in particular applications than it is as a general statement. For example, Milton's poetry for the most part takes the form of *myth*; Donne's the form of *metaphor* and *image*. And translating the distinction into the form of the drama, the *myth* will correspond with the plot, *metaphor* and *image* with the diction. In the Greek drama, the poetry for the most part took the first form, and the practice became a principle with Aristotle: "It is evident from the above that the poet must be more the poet of his stories than of his verses, inasmuch as he is poet by virtue of the imitative element in his work, and it is actions that he imitates".[1]

The Elizabethan drama at its best allows of both forms at once. Shakespeare, in all his greatest plays, has poetry of plot, *myth*, and poetry of verses, of *metaphor* and *image*. In this, more than

[1] *Poet.* 9. It should be remembered that the Greek word for "plot" is actually the word μῦθος. It would be interesting to investigate the exact relation between the two meanings.

in any other clear distinction which might be made, lies his superiority over the Greek dramatists.

But the poetry of *metaphor* and *image* is hardly compatible with a great degree of realism, for it must inevitably remove the diction far from that of everyday life. And so, if the realistic dramatist is to be poetic,[1] his poetry must be of the first type, in the plot. It is for this reason that Heywood fails to achieve realism, where *Arden* achieves it. Heywood commits the double error of using poor plots,[2] and of admitting too much metaphor and image into his diction.[3] *Arden*, on the other hand, has a really poetic plot; the way in which Arden escapes death by accident over and over again, until one almost feels that he is fated to live in spite of his wife, is a truly mythic

[1] And, as we shall see, he cannot be a dramatist if he is not poetic in some way.

[2] This hardly needs illustration. An exception is, perhaps, the plot of *The English Traveller*, which is, however, ruined by a vile under-plot, and minor mismanagements of all kinds.

[3] E.g. Wendoll's speech in Act v, sc. 3, of *A Woman Killed with Kindness*—"Pursued with horror of a guilty soul..."; the long speech of Young Lionel in the first act of *The English Traveller*: "To what may young men best compare themselves...".

creation[1]; there are few plays in which one is made to feel the force of destiny so vividly, and yet so subtly. And the diction is plain to baldness, with a minimum of departure from everyday speech even in the verse passages. As Francklin says in the Epilogue:

Gentlemen, we hope youle pardon this naked Tragedy,
Wherein no filed points are foisted in
To make it gratious to the eare or eye;
For simple trueth is gratious enough,
And needes no other points of glosing stuffe.

It is, indeed, a true description of the play, and the style of the apology is as good an example of the prosiness of the verse as one could find.

Thus it seems that the realistic effect is to be achieved by putting the poetry in the right place, and not by a complete absence of poetry. We shall find confirmation of this in later work, and for the moment, we may leave this aspect of the domestic drama of the Elizabethan age.

One other thing remains to be discussed in this connection. The events represented in the plays of Heywood and in *Arden* are hardly to be described as events of daily life. Murders of

[1] It makes no difference that the author took the hint of this from the account in Holinshed's *Chronicle*.

[61]

husbands by wives, and piteous happenings such as those of *A Woman Killed with Kindness*, are, fortunately, rare. Is it necessary to add a proviso to our notion of the realistic drama that the events represented, like the characters and the diction, must be such as one would commonly find in everyday life? In practice, it does not seem that such a provision is necessary. In effect, it would mean simply that comic plots are more realistic than tragic ones, since, on the whole, men find many more things amusing than they find tragic. And if we examine plays of both kinds from various periods, it does not seem that the tragic rareness of the event makes for loss of realism as compared with comedy. For example, the most realistic of the Elizabethan comedies, such as Jonson's *Bartholomew Fair* and Dekker's *Shoemaker's Holiday*, approximate no more nearly to real life than does *Arden*. Indeed, it often happens that in the tragic events, the dramatist finds enough interest without adding any allurements in the way of complications of plot and turns of speech, whereas the comedian must make common events amusing by the addition of unlikely intrigues and unrealistic jests.

On the whole, we may conclude that the events

of the realistic play need not be events of every-day life: that it is enough if the audience may feel that "if this were to happen to me (which is very unlikely) it would happen obviously very much in this way". Such, probably, would be the feeling of the average contemporary audience of *Arden*; it was not likely that their wives were plotting to kill them, but if they were to do so, it would happen very much in the way in which Alice plotted to kill Arden.

Yet this use of rare events, of murders and sudden deaths, is another great difference between the domestic drama and the realistic drama as we conceive it to-day. For the modern drama generally tries to use the events of every-day life as its material, and to get its effects by a kind of innuendo, or a use of symbolism which makes the small things represent the great things. In this respect, more than in any other, we see that even the writers of the domestic drama in the Elizabethan period were under the influence of the category of tragedy. And it is by comparison with them in this respect that we see exactly how far the writers of the nineteenth century had escaped from the same category.

CHAPTER V

THE NEO-CLASSIC PERIOD

I. THEORY

By the Neo-Classic period, I mean the seventeenth and eighteenth centuries, in all countries, and also a good deal of Italian theory and practice which, though it was actually anterior to the great creative periods of England and Spain in the sixteenth century, still belongs ideally to the Neo-Classic period, when it had its full effect. The greater part of the work of Ben Jonson also seems to be better regarded as part of Neo-Classicism than as Elizabethan.

In the theory of this period, we are concerned chiefly, of course, with the development of Aristotelian doctrine into the systems of the Three Unities, and so forth. In this development, the chief part was played by Castelvetro, who, it is generally recognised, first supplied a reasoned account of the Unities, based on a conception of the actual conditions of dramatic presentation. In Aristotle, as we have noticed,[1] the

[1] *Vide* p. 9.

Unities are but loosely and vaguely formulated, and no explicit reason is advanced for adhering to them; they are nothing more than observations on the actual practice of the Greek dramatists. And in most of the Aristotelian scholars of the Renaissance, to whom drama was not a thing performed, but a thing read in the closet, even this element of justification was lost, and the Unities became one of the most notorious dogmas in the history of art.

According to Castelvetro, the rules of dramatic art must be deduced from the actual conditions of the stage, which are briefly these: the theatre is a public place, in which a play is presented before an audience of ordinary persons, upon a circumscribed platform, and in a limited space of time. From the fact that the stage is one place, the Unity of place follows, and similarly the Unity of time from the fact that the audience can only stay in the theatre for a certain time. Both deductions depend upon what is really an extreme conception of realism—that the events represented must be as nearly alike as is possible to the actual events which they represent, supposing that these actual events were happening on the stage. This notion was expressed in the word *verisimile*, or *vraisemblable*,[1] which becomes almost too familiar to the student of the dramatic literature of the Neo-Classic period.

It may well be asked how, in view of this conception, the use of verse was defended. Castelvetro managed to make it quite consistent with the rest of his theory by pointing out that verse permitted the actors to raise their voices so that they might be heard in the distant parts of the theatre, and that prose would not allow them to do this. This account was by no means universally accepted, and the question was the occasion of one of the most profitable of the controversies of the period in England—that between Dryden and Howard.

But in general outline, Castelvetro's views were widely held, and provided the basis for the speculations on the Unities which occupied the critics so largely in the seventeenth century. In the large body of material which accumulated on this subject, there is little to be learnt concerning

[1] If we are to assign this notion to any one source, it will be to the line of Horace which we have already quoted: "Ficta voluptatis causa sint proxima veris". The theory of the *verisimile* itself is associated particularly with the elder Scaliger, but is common to almost all the critics of the period, Italian, French, English and German.

the question of realism. Among the French, there is nothing to help us; only Corneille stands outside the orthodoxy based on Castelvetro, and his views are, for all their ingenuity, no more than an attempt to show that his own departures from the rules may be easily reconciled with the rules. Among the Germans, the earlier writers, such as Fabricius and Opitz, add nothing to the orthodox views, and the later, such as Lessing, show little advance in the understanding of realism. Only in England, it seems, was any real contribution made, as we have said, in the dispute between Dryden and Howard.

But leaving aside, for the moment, any discussion of specific doctrines, the criticism of the period is certainly the clearest example which we could give of the way in which forms of expression may be so rigidly defined by the critics that they unduly restrict the freedom of artistic creation. The circumstances which made this possible are very complicated, and we need hardly enter into them in detail here. Chief among them was certainly the widespread adoption of a rationalistic attitude to life, and to all subjects of speculation, irrespective of whether they were such as can be dealt with by rational methods. It was with good reason that Boileau said "Descartes has cut the throat of poetry"; and yet we must notice that, however clearly Boileau may have realised this, he did nothing to help matters, but accepted the Cartesian attitude so firmly that it was largely through his influence that poetry was allowed to bleed to death. Indeed, no one seems to have been capable of any remedial attempt. The artists themselves were so much a part of the culture in which they lived (how should they not be?) that they accepted the dicta of criticism almost without a struggle, and their work exhibited a sort of spontaneous contraction even before the critics imposed harsher limits upon it. The full extent of the capitulation is evident only when we examine the actual works of the period.

To some degree, the effects of rationalism were augmented by the fact that the civilisation of the period was urban, mercantile, bourgeois. There has never been a period in which the rural elements of the population counted for less, and it is from these elements, from the peasants, and from those in close contact with the peasants, that the deepest material of art has always come. Mythology, in fact, is always rural, is discovered and fostered by those who are in close contact with Nature and her operations—who are, in fact, compelled to struggle with an environment which is inexplicable save by mythological, religious, or poetical methods. An urban population, on the other hand, is accustomed only to the works of man, to the material evidence of the achievement of man in the control of Nature, and so more easily accepts a rationalistic interpretation of experience. It is unnecessary to point out here the complete absence of any rural influence in the literature of Neo-Classicism; the fact is notorious, and it is not hard to see how it is connected with the rationalistic, rather arrogant, attitude to Nature which is so much opposed to the imaginative and mythological attitudes natural to poetry.

A more precise result of this urban character of the culture of the period was that the poet addressed himself to an audience of some education, which was itself to some extent governed by the critics; so that purely critical preconceptions were of more importance in this period than in any other. Altogether, it is not to be wondered at that the drama of the seventeenth and eighteenth centuries is what it is. But it remains nevertheless a warning of the results of allowing too much influence to the critics,[1] and perhaps the best that can be said for it is that it may prevent the recurrence of a similar mistake.

So much for the general character of the theory of the period with which we are dealing. Let us return now to minor questions, in which, fortunately, we can give a better report of it.

In the first place, the general discussion of the question of the Unities had at least the result of raising the problem of dramatic illusion, and by some authors this problem was brought to a very satisfactory formulation, if not to a conclusion. Dryden, especially, deals with it in a most ingenious manner, in the *Defence of an Essay of Dramatic Poesy*.[2] There he is concerned to refute Howard's contention[3] that the improbability of making a stage represent two countries is not

[1] It is remarkable that the most typical figures of the period, Boileau and Dr Johnson, were critics primarily, and only secondarily poets, even in their own day; while to-day we inevitably think of both as critics only.

[2] I should perhaps add that in the *Essay* itself there is nothing so much to our purpose as the passage quoted below, and I do not consider it necessary to undertake any examination of it.

[3] For the details of this controversy, I refer the reader to Mr Arundell's *Dryden and Howard*, Cambridge, 1929.

greater than that of making it represent two houses, because there are no degrees of improbability. His main position is that the imagination, and not the reason, is the judge of matters on the stage, and that improbabilities, however they may be all equal to the reason, are not equal to the imagination:

...'tis proved that a stage may properly represent two rooms or two houses; for the imagination being judge of what is represented, will in reason be less shocked with the appearance of two rooms in the same house, or two houses in the same city, than with two distant cities in the same country, or two remote countries in the same universe. Imagination in a man, or reasonable creature, is supposed to participate of reason, and when that governs, as it does in the belief of fiction, Reason is not destroyed, but misled or blinded; that can prescribe to the Reason, during the time of the representation, somewhat like a weak belief of what it sees and hears; and Reason suffers itself to be so hoodwinked, that it may better enjoy the pleasures of the fiction: but is never so wholly made captive, as to be drawn headlong into a persuasion of those things which are most remote from possibility: 'tis in that case a free-born subject, not a slave; it will contribute willingly its assent, as far as it sees convenient, but it will not be forced.[1]

[1] *Essays of John Dryden*, ed. Ker, vol. 1, p. 127.

[71]

It seems to me that one could hardly hope for a better definition of the nature of dramatic illusion than this, unless it were to be achieved by an exact psychological analysis which we can hardly expect until the science of psychology has advanced considerably beyond the point that it has now reached. As a reasonable, non-technical account of the matter, Dryden's seems to me in no way inferior to that of Coleridge, which we may quote here for the sake of comparison:

These, and all other stage presentations, are to produce a sort of temporary half-faith, which the spectator encourages in himself, and supports by a voluntary contribution on his own part, because he knows that it is at all times in his power to see the thing as it really is....The true stage-illusion in this and in all other things consists—not in the mind's judging it to be a forest, but, in its remission of the judgement that it is not a forest.[1]

[1] *Progress of the Drama*. The description of dramatic illusion here has obvious affinities with the formula which Coleridge gives for the state of mind of the reader of poetry—"the suspension of disbelief". There has been a great deal of argument recently concerning this question of poetry and belief (by Dr Richards, Mr Eliot, and others); if any conclusion is reached in this question, it can hardly fail to throw light on the subject of dramatic illusion. But at the moment it is not possible to employ the discussion profitably for this purpose.

There is obviously a general agreement here with the views of Dryden, and, as I have said, I see no reason to suppose that we may discover any better account of the subject without making use of technical psychology. And since technical psychology cannot, at the moment, do anything for us, we must be content to leave the matter where Dryden and Coleridge left it. Dramatic illusion—the judgment of the audience on the reality of the events represented—is not, as the theorists of the Unities supposed, a complete delusion; the members of the audience do not believe that what they see is actually happening, but neither do they, as Dr Johnson maintained,[1] remain in a firm conscious belief that what they see is not really happening, but is merely a stage presentation; the actual frame of mind is somewhere between the two—a sort of half-belief, in which the reason allows itself, with some reservations and wariness, to be deceived by the imagination.

There is one other aspect of the quarrel between Dryden and Howard which concerns us—the dispute over the use of rhyme, which Dryden had defended in the *Essay*, and which he

[1] *Preface to Shakespeare.*

defends again in the *Defence* against the attacks of Howard. Howard, I should say, seems to me to be one of those rather obscure figures who have suffered a neglect which, though regrettable, is very easily understood. The extent of his critical work is only three or four pages: something much shorter than the shortest of Dryden's Prefaces. Yet, in this small space, he says more that is to the point than one finds in any similar number of pages of Dryden; particularly he is significant as a writer who was definitely thwarted, and knew that he was being thwarted, by the rules and forms laid down by the critics. His Preface to his play *The Duke of Lerma* is, in this way, one of the most pathetic documents of the period, but its pathos is enlivened by some excellent hits at the oppressors.

In the matter of rhymed verse, Howard gives a most remarkable definition of the attitude of the audience to a play: "Now after all the Endeavours of that ingenious Person, a Play will still be supposed to be a Composition of several Persons speaking *ex tempore*".[1] That there is a great deal of truth in this will be recognised by anyone who has suffered from actors who do not

[1] *The Duke of Lerma*: To the Reader.

[74]

know their parts. Mere bad acting, incompetent producing, or ill-designed scenery, will never destroy the illusion as completely as the voice of the prompter. And words spoken at a great pace seem to destroy the illusion in the same way, because they force upon the mind the conviction that the actor has learnt them,—that he cannot possibly be speaking *ex tempore*. Howard himself uses his discovery (for it is a discovery) to prove the superiority of blank verse to rhymed verse,[1] but the same principle, if logically applied, would lead us inevitably to the conclusion that prose is, for the great majority of plays, the most realistic medium.[2]

The main object of Howard's little essay is to protest against the way in which the critics had

[1] With engaging ingenuousness he admits freely that his own practice does not conform with this principle; he writes rhymed or blank verse indifferently, as he says, just as the fancy took him.

[2] I say in most plays, because it is just possible that there are some passions and feelings which may be more realistically represented in verse than in prose. For example, most lovers would be very willing to address their mistresses in verse if they could, and it would be highly appropriate if they were to do so. And a representation may be realistic by presenting, not what people do, but what they imagine themselves as doing, in this way.

[75]

affected the taste of the public, and persuaded them to accept rules and forms which were only made by the application of Reason in an improper way:

In the next place, I must ingenuously confess, that the manner of Plays, which are now in most esteem, is beyond my power to perform; nor do I condemn in the least anything of what Nature soever that pleases; since nothing could appear to me a ruder folly, than to censure the Satisfaction of others: I rather blame the unnecessary Understanding of some that have labour'd to give strict Rules to Things that are not Mathematical, and with such eagerness, pursuing their own seeming Reasons, that at last we are to apprehend such Argumentative *Poets* will grow as strict as *Sancho Panco's* Doctor was to our very appetites; for in the difference of Tragedy and Comedy, and of Farce itself, there can be no determination but by the Taste.[1]

This, whether it be just or not, is very much what any modern critic would say on the subject: and indeed is very much what Professor Saintsbury has said on it, at greater length. It is only to

[1] This use of the word "taste", for taste in art, "le bon goût", was very new at the time, and had not come into general use in England. It is derived from the Spanish critic Gracian, and it is perhaps significant that Howard associates it with Spanish literature here.

be regretted that Howard gave up the struggle so easily, though it may be doubted whether the efforts of any one person could have overthrown the orthodox views that Tragedy and Comedy were things as essentially and really separate as Good and Evil, or White and Black. And, after all, Howard's suggestion is hardly a theory—is really only one of those sudden *aperçus* which may be thrown out by a writer who, in the main, accepts the current views.

No doubt many such suggestions might be unearthed in other writers of the period: in the *Discours* of Corneille, and in the *Examens* which follow most of his tragedies, in the works of Saint Évremond, and other theorists of the seventeenth century; or later, in the critical works of Voltaire,[1] and his contemporaries in Germany. But, at any rate on the scale of the present work, it is doubtful if the search is worth undertaking with any care, and whether the results obtained by even a casual attempt are worth reporting.

So I will conclude our account of Neo-Classic

[1] It is always a temptation to quote his dictum on Shakespeare from the *Lettres Philosophiques*; we need only add here that it might well stand for any English orthodox of the same period.

[77]

theory with two authors, one of whom, Rymer, may be supposed to be the most extreme exponent of the orthodox theories (so extreme that he even becomes unorthodox), and the other, Diderot, who points forward to the new type of drama.

Thomas Rymer has acquired a certain notoriety for his attacks on the Elizabethans, and too often it has not been understood that he was actuated by the very best motives, and that his theories deserve serious consideration. The following passage, from the attack on *Othello*, represents the extreme development of the theory of *types*, which was originally part of the theory of comedy, but which was transferred to tragedy in the Renaissance:[1]

Philosophy tells us it is a principle in the Nature of Man *to be grateful*.

History may tell us that *John an Oakes, John a Stiles*, or *Jago* were ungrateful; *Poetry* is to follow Nature; Philosophy must be his guide: history and *fact* in particular instances of *John an Oakes* or *John of Styles*, are no warrant or direction for a poet. Therefore Aristotle is always saying that Poetry is σπουδαιότερον καὶ φιλοσοφώτερον, is more general and abstracted,

[1] What we have described in our chapter on Roman Comedy as the stylisation of character.

is led more by Philosophy, the reason and nature of things, than History: which only records things higlety piglety, right or wrong as they happen. History might without preamble or difficulty, say that Jago was ungrateful. Philosophy then calls him unnatural....

To entertain the Audience with something new and surprising, against common sense and Nature, he (i.e. Shakespeare) would pass upon us a close, dissembling, false, insinuating rascal, instead of an open-hearted, frank, plain-dealing Souldier, a character constantly worn by them for some thousands of years in the world....[1]

This view of dramatic characters as types takes us further away from realism than any other theory. It substitutes symbols for people, and precludes every possibility of realism in the development of character, which must always tend to present the individual in his greatest individuality, as he is in life. And yet we may notice that it springs from a theory which was intended to produce the greatest possible effect of credibility, of vraisemblance: there could be no better illustration of the errors into which the Neo-Classical critics fell through adherence to the view that the drama must aim at complete delusion.

[1] *Short View of Tragedy*, ch. v.

In close contrast with this view of Rymer's, I would place certain passages of Diderot, in which the notion of a truly realistic drama is adumbrated:

En cet endroit, Dorval s'écria: "O toi qui possédes toute la chaleur du génie à une âge où il reste à peine aux autres une froide raison, que ne puis-je être à tes côtés, ton Euménide? je t'agiterais sans relâche. Tu le ferais, cet ouvrage; je te rappellerais les larmes que nous a fait répandre la scène de l'Enfant prodigue et de son valet; et en disparaissant d'entre nous, tu ne nous laisserais pas le regret d'un genre dont tu pouvais être le fondateur".

— Et ce genre, comment l'appellerez-vous?

— La tragédie domestique et bourgeoise. Les Anglais ont le Marchand de Londres[1] et le Joueur, tragédies en prose. Les tragédies de Shakespeare sont moitié vers et moitié prose. Le premier poéte qui nous fit rire avec de la prose, introduisit la prose dans la comédie. Le premier poéte qui nous fera pleurer avec de la prose, introduira la prose dans la Tragédie.

Mais dans l'art, ainsi que dans la Nature, tout est enchaîné; si l'on se rapproche d'un côté de ce qui est vrai, on s'en rapprochera de beaucoup d'autres; c'est alors que nous verrons sur la scène des situations naturelles, qu'une décence ennemie du génie et des grands effets a proscrites.[2]

[1] Lillo's *George Barnwell*.
[2] *Entretiens sur le Fils Naturel*, 2.

Here we have a clear suggestion of the
realistic drama, and it is interesting to notice that
Diderot considered that it could only be achieved
by disregarding the rules of his day. A little later
he says more of the *genre sérieux*, as he calls it, and
points out that it would lie midway between the
comic and the tragic:

C'est l'avantage du genre sérieux, que, placé entre
les deux autres, il a des ressources, soit qu'il s'élève,
soit qu'il descende. Il n'en est pas ainsi du genre
comique et du genre tragique: toutes les nuances du
comique sont comprises entre ce genre même et le
genre sérieux; et toutes celles du tragiques, le bur-
lesque, et le merveilleux, sont également hors de la
nature....Pour un homme de goût, il y a la même
absurdité dans Castor élevé au rang des dieux, et dans
le Bourgeois gentilhomme, fait Mamamouchi....
C'est dans le genre sérieux, que doit s'exercer d'abord
tout homme de lettres qui se sent du talent pour la
scène.[1]

Here is interesting enough confirmation of
much that we have said on the subject of tragedy
and comedy. But the reader will be disappointed
if he turns to the plays of Diderot to find the same
principles put into practice: that was not for his
age to perform.

[1] *Ibid.* 3.

II. NEO-CLASSICAL PRACTICE

The practice of this period we can dismiss briefly. Tragedy, based on a rigid notion and definition of the form, was completely unrealistic in style, in characters, in plot, and in construction. Even the limited and peculiar realism of the historical play was absent, for very few historical plays were written: plays, that is, on subjects taken from the history of the author's own country. Of the less obvious kind of historical play, on themes taken from the history of other countries, there were enough and more than enough, but generally they departed even further from realism than the plays on purely fictitious events.[1] Often adherence to a mistaken set of rules intended to produce complete delusion, led to a degree of disillusion, if we may use the word in this sense, which is to be found in the drama of no other period; Corneille's *Le Cid* may serve as an example of this.

[1] It was often observed that the characters of Racine's historical plays were so far from being Roman or Greek that upon the first appearance of each of them, the public amused itself by discovering figures in the contemporary world from whom its persons were drawn.

Comedy, governed by a similar rigid definition, departed even further from the speech and
action of real life. In England, at the Restoration, it became the vehicle of a kind of wit both
in speech and in action which is very far removed from the events of ordinary life, and
in the eighteenth century the same tradition
was developed. Even the plays of Goldsmith
fall within the same category, although in some
respects they show a slightly greater approximation to realism.

In France, comedy, taking its cue from
Molière, turned to a species of satire and intrigue
which involved continual improbabilities, and
depended more and more on the type-character,
such as *le bourgeois Gentilhomme*, *Tartuffe*, *l'Avare*;
it became, in fact, less and less a mirror of life,
and more and more a comment upon life of an
indirect kind.

The species of tragedy and comedy were kept
so distinct that the tragi-comedy of the period,
always advanced by its authors with a sort of
apology for its existence, was constructed in a
manner very unlikely to overcome the disadvantages of its birth. Dryden's tragi-comedies,
for example, keep the comic parts severely

[83]   6-2

separate from the tragic,[1] and although they are, so he tells us, modelled on the Shakespearian drama, they quite miss the point of Shakespeare's use of the comic parts as a device to add to the realism of the tragic.

Yet in spite of the sharp theoretical distinction between the two forms, and the current disdain of tragi-comedy, it is noticeable that the real differences between the tragic manner and the comic manner were often but weakly felt. Surely in a real tragedy, the spectator must be aware almost from the first moment that he is in a tragic atmosphere, and nowhere near comedy? But it was possible for Howard to write *The Vestal Virgin* as a tragedy, and to add to it an alternative fourth and fifth act which turned it into a comedy!

There is one, and only one, writer of domestic plays in the tradition of the Elizabethans, George Lillo, whose *George Barnwell* was a great success: was translated into French, German, and Dutch, earned the praise of Diderot and Lessing, who

[1] Dryden considered that the function of the comic portions was simply to provide relief for the audience; naturally, then, they were kept quite separate. *Vide* the quotation from the *Essay* on p. 42.

modelled on it his own *Miss Sarah Sampson*. If this play is compared with *Arden*,[1] it is obvious at once that Lillo almost destroys the realism which he might have achieved by his choice of plot, through a too open moralising, and a patent desire to instruct rather than to reproduce. As in the comedy of the period, he was not content to let the audience draw their own conclusions concerning the actions which he dealt with, but must thrust under the noses of his hearers his own opinions.

This, indeed, was the most general fault of all the drama of the Neo-Classic period. In one way or another, the dramatist himself was always present in the mouths of his actors, either by judgments on moral questions, by satire, by wit, or by "fine writing". There never was a period in which plays were less "compositions of various persons speaking *ex tempore*", as Howard would have had them. And this characteristic, obviously contrary to all possibility of realistic effect, was a direct consequence of the undue

[1] Which, by the way, Lillo rewrote in his own manner, so that an exact comparison is possible. Incidentally, Lillo's use of *Arden* is an interesting proof of the position held by the play in English as the great example of domestic drama.

dominance of criticism. The artist and his
audience were both made self-conscious, about
themselves, and about the play. The only gleam
of realism lay in the fact that most of them were
self-conscious about life too. But the two blacks
do not make a white.

There remains just one qualification for this
opinion. As we have already hinted, it is possible
that an artist may accommodate himself to the
rules so happily that they do not interfere with
him: or rather, he may make them so much part
of his outlook that he follows them naturally,
unconsciously, and so hardly seems to follow
them at all. In our period there is the one great
example of Racine. His genius, so much gentler
than that of Corneille, submitted itself to the
rules without any effort, and he was able to produce some plays which are completely in accordance with the Unities and all the principles of his
teachers. In particular, there is the *Bérénice*,
which represents an action taking place in one
room, and in a period of time almost exactly
equal to the representation. Personally, I find
that the play does achieve a peculiar kind of
realism, and I can only explain it by the fact
that it does all that the critics wanted it to

do.[1] And so it may well be that the real objection to the Unities was not that they were wrong in principle, but that they were too hard to practise. I am unwilling to believe that: but the achievement of Racine very nearly persuades me to it.

[1] Among the plays of the ancients, I find the same effect only in the *Philoctetes*.

CHAPTER VI

THE NINETEENTH CENTURY

I. THEORY

(a) *General Survey*

THE break-up of Neo-Classicism was the result partly of its own decadence, and partly of the growth of the new movement which we call Romanticism. We must now try to discover whether there was anything in Romanticism which prepared the way for realism.

The definition or description of Romanticism is, of course, no easy matter, and our account of it must take into consideration some notion of Classicism, to which it is commonly opposed. In general, it is hard to find a better description than that given by T. E. Hulme, and to this we shall refer in our use of the words. According to Hulme, Classicism and Romanticism each spring from a fairly clear attitude towards human nature; Classicism regards man as naturally base, animal, and uncivilised, and holds that only by discipline can he attain to his proper humanity and civilisation. Thus discipline, in all forms and in all spheres, is the mark of Classicism; in art particularly, it manifests itself in a close concern with form, with high finish, and with the avoidance of all kinds of violence and over-emphasis which spring from lack of discipline. Romanticism, on the other hand, assumes that man is naturally noble, but that he is dragged down and debased by the various forms of discipline which he has invented—by Society, by morality, by law, and so forth. Thus the opening words of Rousseau's *Contrat Social*, "Mankind is born free, but finds himself everywhere in chains", are the first great expression of Romanticism in Europe. In art, then, Romanticism consists in the rejection of all forms and definitions, and in a reliance on the sheer unhampered free expression of the artists.

It is not hard to see that, if we can accept this description, Romanticism embraced within itself the principles of realism. In the method of approach to the subject, it is freer and more direct; if the Romantic writer wishes to approach nature, he need not, as Rymer insisted the Classical writer should, use Philosophy as his guide—he need not, in fact, use any kind of

[89]

discipline, but may observe it and report his impressions without any kind of modification or reservation. And in the form of his art, he is not bound by categories, as the Classical writer is, but may evolve for every work which he does a new form. In the drama, at least, he was free from the notions of tragedy and comedy in their absolute sense, and need only use them as far as they happened to suit his purpose. We have seen already that the realistic type of drama tends to take the form of a middle term between tragedy and comedy, dealing with people neither worse nor better than ourselves, and the freedom of form which came with Romanticism helps to make this possible.

The realistic tendencies of Romanticism in its early stages are well illustrated in the poetry of Wordsworth, and in his doctrine that the diction of poetry should be a selection of the language used by real men. But in this respect, Wordsworth is something of an exception, and the general tendency of the Romantic movement was to develop a kind of writing which was far removed from realism, and in the typical Romantic drama of Hugo, speech, action, and sentiments are all as unrealistic as they may be.[1] Throughout the century, these two aspects of Romanticism seem to exist quite happily, side by side. In the first half, the more poetic and passionate aspect prevailed, and in the second half, the realistic attitude took its place. The reason for this change we must examine in some detail.

(b) Poetry, Science and Pessimism

It is noticeable that many of the critical documents which we have examined in this essay so far, connect the drama very closely with poetry. Aristotle's treatise, indeed, is entitled "The Poetics", and not "The Dramatics"; and the period of the Neo-Classics faithfully followed his example, as in Dryden's *Essay on Dramatick Poesy*. And we have already referred to the discussions on the subject of the merits of rhymed verse, blank verse, and prose in the drama. Perhaps the most striking thing about the drama of the late nineteenth century was its rejection of

[1] It is remarkable that both of the great periods of the drama in France open with a Spanish play—Corneille's *Le Cid* in the seventeenth century, and Hugo's *Hernani* in the nineteenth century. Spain has always signified to the French a kind of escape from their own rather unpoetic attitude to life:—as in their proverbial saying "châteaux en Espagne".

the poetic, in certain plays by certain authors, completely and consciously. In this, more than in anything else, the realism of the modern drama would seem to consist, and we must inquire, first why it was done, then how it was done, and finally, whether it was really done at all.

The clue to the reason why it was done we find in the well-known passage of Coleridge on the nature of poetry in the introductory Lecture to Shakespeare. We may quote the essential parts of it, but no selection can really stand for the whole argument, which includes an entire theory of the nature of poetry, and indeed, in a compressed form, a whole theory of aesthetics. "Poetry is not the proper antithesis to prose, but to science. Poetry is opposed to science, and prose to metre. The proper and immediate object of science is the acquirement or communication of truth; the proper and immediate object of poetry is the communication of immediate pleasure." There are, of course, additions to be made to this statement, but for our present purpose this will serve.

"Poetry is opposed to science": the rejection of poetry by the realists of the nineteenth century was part of an attempt to introduce into literature the methods of science, detached observation, suppression of the opinions of the observer, and a faithful report of the plain truth. Thus Zola, in the most important critical document of realism in the theatre,[1] claims that his object is not the "communication of pleasure", but "a wider and wider grasp of the truth":

Aujourd'hui, nos chimistes sont partis de l'étude de la nature, et s'ils trouvent jamais la fabrication de l'or, ce sera par une méthode scientifique. Je suis comme eux. J'emploie et je tâche simplement de perfectionner la méthode moderne qui doit nous conduire à la possession de plus en plus vaste de la vérité.

This passage will serve as our text for the theory of realism in the nineteenth century; no better could be found. It exhibits the attachment to the methods of science, derived from a natural, though perhaps misguided admiration for the results of experimental science. There is the significant emphasis on "method": significant because, as even Zola discovered, only the method of science can be applied to art, which must always remain art, and can never adopt the true mental attitude of science. And there is the equally significant use of the word "modern"—

[1] *Le Naturalisme au Théâtre*, p. 175.

"the modern method". European culture, since the Renaissance at any rate, seems to have been distinguished from all other cultures, ancient and modern, by a development of the passion for novelty, and an author has only to claim for himself the discovery of something new to gain a respectful hearing, apart from any other merits of his work. As Dr Brandes says: "That which above all interests us in a poet of the present day is the new thought that comes to life in him. Our first question is: 'Where lies his discovery? what is his America?'" Dr Brandes took this very much for granted. As, indeed, he well might in a century which believed firmly in the idea of progress in all its various forms. But his assumption would have appeared very curious among the Chinese, among the ancient Greeks and Romans, or even among Europeans of the Middle Ages.

It is to this same belief in progress that Zola's use of the word "modern" appeals, and to which every modernist revolution in the arts owes its success. When we add that the notion of progress is essentially associated with the theory that science will necessarily continue to increase the sum of human knowledge, and the possibilities of human conquest in the world of Nature, then we see that Zola's double appeal to modernism and to scientific method is a formidable matter, and we can well understand the way in which realism succeeded Romanticism as "the new thing".

But when we come to consider how this revolution of theory was put into practice, difficulties arise. At the outset, there is the fact that the worlds of science and of poetry, or art in its most general sense, are essentially separate. The communication of truth, and the communication of pleasure, are never to be achieved by the same means; a scientific diagram is not a painting, a description of plants by a botanist is not a Georgic, and a faithful reproduction of a scene from real life on the stage would not be realistic drama, if it were really a faithful reproduction, and nothing more. All these things might, of course, produce a certain pleasure, but the pleasure is only incidental to their main purpose of communicating truth, and is derived rather from the neatness or cleverness with which they do this. In a word, the pleasure is not in the thing itself, in the matter, but in the technique. In just the same way, the public of the more uninstructed kind used to prefer Paganini's "farmyard imitations" to his serious music. There will always be a legitimate pleasure in technique alone, but the serious admirer of any art will always take great pains to distinguish it from the pleasure arising from art itself.

This consideration precludes the possibility of the most absolute kind of realism—a completely faithful representation of an actual scene upon the stage. For example, the ideal realistic drama would consist simply in the appearance of the actors on a stage completely free from decoration of any kind; they would speak *ex tempore*, and would say anything which appeared to them necessary—would probably comment on the audience, and on the reasons which had induced them to appear before it. This would be complete realism: the drama would actually *be* the state of affairs in the theatre itself. But clearly it would not be art.

Zola himself seems to have realised that the drama can never attain this completely scientific ideal: that it must, if it is to be drama, a form of art, include other, non-scientific elements. In one place, where he is a little off his guard, he goes so far as to admit that realism has a kind of poetry of its own: "On trouvera la formule, on arrivera à prouver qu'il y a plus de poésie dans le petit appartement d'un ouvrier que dans tous les palais vides et vermoulus de l'histoire".[1]

The truth is, that the realists did not use science itself, but introduced into their work an attitude, a philosophy, which was, until recently, invariably associated with science—*pessimism*. Apart from the complicated philosophic doctrines with which it has been decorated, pessimism is a simple enough attitude. It is only one of many systems which endeavour to satisfy the need which mankind feels for prevision, for knowledge of the future, in this world, or in the next. The particular modification called pessimism is based on a remarkable mechanism, which is perhaps best shown in a Portuguese proverb directed actually against pessimism, which says "The worst is not the surest". For the pessimist agrees with himself that the worst shall be the surest, he will always expect the worst. This gives him an odd kind of prevision, which provides for all eventualities. If the worst happens—if things turn out as he pretended to know that they would, then he is justified, and the justification provided for the general theory by the most acute

[1] *Op. cit.*

miseries will in some measure even compensate him for his sufferings. On the other hand, if things turn out better than he had expected, then at least there is a pleasant surprise, and the worse he expected things to be, the more likely he is to find a number of things turning out rather better than worse. Thus, as one might suppose, pessimism, like most opposites, proves to be very much the same thing as its antithesis optimism. It cannot really be said that one is a truer view of life than the other, for from a detached point of view —the point of view, for example, of a statistician, it is fairly certain that human events would prove to be partly good, partly evil, and partly indifferent, with the middle category as the largest, and nothing much to choose between the other two.

But there is a further consideration: that men commonly connect what they fear with reality, and what they hope with illusion. At whatever stage of human history one chooses to examine this, it will be seen that it is true. Primitive man, indeed, seems to have been originally without any symbols of hope; all his gods were gods of fear, of forces arrayed against him, and modern students of the primitive mentality agree that this supernatural world of fear is much more real to the savage even than his own daily life.[1] It is only comparatively late in human development that symbols of hope are found, and they are generally soon associated with illusion, with idealism in philosophy, as opposed to the materialistic, realistic systems which depend on the conviction of reality based on fear.

It is for this reason, I think, that we find everywhere the feeling that tragedy, the play with the unhappy ending, is more "real" than comedy, even in spite of the fact that, according to all theoretical standards, comedy is much more like life itself than is tragedy.

We need not insist on the importance of the scientific discoveries of the nineteenth century in augmenting this pessimist realism. Darwin's theory of the survival of the fittest was perhaps the most striking example of it, but the general tendency of science was to present the world as completely inhuman, and to maintain that events in the life of man are predetermined as links in a chain of causes and effects which, in turn, is part of an irrational, but determined universe. In the

[1] *La Mentalité Primitive*, and *Les Fonctions Mentales dans les Sociétés Inférieures*. Lévy-Bruhl.

face of such a picture, and in the breaking up of the old theological systems, men were thrown back once more on the primitive fear in the face of nature; and they feared the worst, because they liked to feel at least that they knew what was going to happen—"the worst is the surest".

So it is that to-day we have this peculiar use of the phrase "the realities of the situation", for the most gloomy view which can possibly be taken: and the natural opposite of this pessimistic view, anything that tends to optimism, is characterised as "idealistic", illusory. The recent disputes over events in the Far East have provided many remarkable instances of this usage.

And it is by the use of a pessimism of this kind that the realist drama, and realist literature in general, is to be distinguished from other literature, if we are to distinguish it at all. Such a distinction, at any rate, would not depend on purely critical and external definitions, but rather on the true spirit of the creative effort. Moreover, it is very doubtful whether we can arrive at a definition on any other grounds. We may say that the realists, freed by the Romantic revolution from the categories imposed in the name of Aristotle on Neo-Classic drama, sought to find a middle way between tragedy and comedy, which should avoid the bias in general attitude and in the characters towards the worse or the better; but, as we shall see, they only achieved this in a limited degree. Or we may take as the basis of our distinction Zola's phrase about the workman's room, and say that realism consisted in dealing with the common people rather than with Kings and Princes. But such a definition will hardly bear examination; the ancient comedy, as we have seen, claimed to deal with people worse than ourselves: Shakespeare makes a special and skilful use of characters from low life—evidently this practice is not peculiar to the realists. Even if we add to this definition the proviso that the dramatist must have a genuine sociological purpose, that he should be democratic, we are only saying that he should involve himself in a particular kind of attitude to life; and, as we shall see, the more sociological drama is, the less is it felt to be realistic. Altogether, we can hardly do more than to insist on the significance of scientific pessimism as the distinctive mark of realism. This seems to be the least arbitrary characteristic of the period, and that which most nearly corresponds with the inner nature of the creative impulse of those writers whom we call realist.

This, then, is our final conclusion in the matter of theory, and I will add here one brief illustration to show how little it is possible to distinguish the principles of nineteenth-century realism from the attempts at realism in the earlier drama. Zola, the most extreme exponent of realism, only makes this claim for himself:

> Il est donc bien entendu que je suis pas assez peu practique pour exiger la copie textuelle de la nature. Je constate uniquement que la tendance paraît être, dans les accessoires, à se rapprocher de la nature le plus possible, et je constate cela comme un symptôme du naturalisme au théâtre.[1]

Compare this with the phrase of Horace:

> Ficta voluptatis causa sint proxima veris:

or with Scaliger's phrase:

> ut quam proxime accedant ad veritatem.

Surely one would have to be a very convinced believer in the necessary progress of the arts to find in Zola any advance on Horace or Scaliger.

---

[1] *Op. cit.* p. 92. The whole passage is of the greatest interest.

II. NINETEENTH-CENTURY PRACTICE

In the greater part of this essay, we have used the word "realism" in a general sense, to indicate the effect of approximation to real life produced on the audience by the play. But in the last few pages, we have obviously passed to another sense of the word, a sense which it acquired through the work of the particular period which we are considering. We have seen, in considering the theory of this school, that it is not easy to define exactly any respect in which they differed from their predecessors, and we must now inquire whether we may draw more useful distinctions from their practice.

We are met at the outset of this inquiry by a very serious difficulty. The movement of realism in the drama was chiefly carried out by writers of other nationalities than English—German, Norwegian, Swedish, Russian and French. Of Norwegian, Russian and Swedish, I know nothing, and my knowledge of German and French is not adequate for this purpose. For obviously if we are to judge the extent of realism of any work, it is of the greatest importance that we should be able to form a fairly exact estimate of the way in which the diction is related to the spoken language. And a knowledge of a foreign language which suffices for all ordinary purposes, will often be insufficient to settle this. A further difficulty arises from the fact that it is in the very nature of realistic drama to introduce minor contemporary fashions in the way of speech which are now out of date,[1] and which present a problem of reconstruction perhaps more difficult than any other; for it is often easier for us to recreate the atmosphere of a period in antiquity than one as near to us as the late nineteenth century. I must admit, then, candidly, that many of the conclusions reached in this part of my essay are very tentative, and my only excuse for offering them is that knowledge of the Scandinavian languages and of Russian is, unhappily, very rare among Englishmen to-day.

Let us take first the case of Zola. Although he was not primarily a playwright, and although his most notable plays are merely modifications of

[1] In our own drama we may notice the way in which some of Wilde's colloquial phrases have become *démodé*, and grate so harshly on the feelings of a modern audience that they are, on the stage, always altered to the contemporary usage. A common example is the phrase "It makes no matter".

[104]

his novels, he deserves consideration as the most famous exponent of realism, and because his example was the starting point of all the other realists; in Germany, indeed, realism was often known as "the French school". Zola's dramas seem to me to suffer from a fault which is found also in his novels—an inability to write lifelike dialogue. In the novels, this is not so serious, and is counterbalanced by his magnificent ability in the description of detail, by his terrible seriousness, and his feeling for the dramatic in the novel-form. But in his dramas, it appears that a writer who has such a feeling for the dramatic in the one form, is not necessarily able to transfer it to the stage. To a certain extent, perhaps, he was hampered by the fact that he was not composing direct for that medium, but only transferring material originally expressed in the form of the novel. But even if he had succeeded in constructing his dramas in a truly dramatic manner, his inability to reproduce the speech of everyday life would have ruined the realistic effect. And as it is, we can only say that Zola serves to show that realism, even in the limited sense in which he conceived it, is only to be achieved by one who has a thorough understanding of the natural rules of dramatic composition. His play on the subject of *Thérèse Raquin* compares unfavourably, in the matter of realistic effect, with *Arden*, dealing with much the same theme, and with the typical "well-made" play of the period, as practised by Sarcey and others like him.

The same might be said, I think, of the realistic plays of Hauptmann, who, writing in German, had an even more difficult task, because in that tongue the written language was traditionally so far removed from the spoken. His plays, otherwise so realistic, make one wonder if it would not be possible for a dramatist to indicate in a purely general way the substance of the various speeches, and leave the actors to fill in the actual words for themselves, in a truly contemporary diction. This would come somewhere near Howard's description of a play as "a composition of several persons speaking *ex tempore*", but it would, of course, place a great responsibility in the hands of the actors—though something of the kind is habitually done in the modern commercial theatre.[1]

[1] This may be observed in the practice of the company which plays farces at the Aldwych Theatre, and has played them there without any long interruption since the War. It is interesting, if one has a good memory, to attend performances of the same play at an interval of

It is noticeable that I do not make a similar complaint of the plays which I am compelled to read in translation. And I fully recognise that if I were able to read them in the original, I might make the same discovery about them too.

There is a further consideration which tends to make me sceptical about my own opinion of the realism of the Russian and Scandinavian plays. In both cases, the average Englishman derives his notion of the way of life of the Russian and Scandinavian peoples from literature, and from literature alone. We have most of us some sort of an idea of how the French live, and how the Germans live, from first-hand knowledge, or from eye-witness reports. But for our knowledge of these other nations, we are almost entirely dependent on books.

Let us take the case of Russia, and particularly as we find it in the works of Tchekov. It is probable that most of us take our notion of the life of Russians under the old regime almost entirely from this writer. Tolstoy, his only rival

several weeks; the changes in the dialogue are astonishing. I have no doubt that the same thing is done in other theatres, though the actors at the Aldwych may be presumed to be more accustomed to it than any other company, through their long association together.

in this sphere, was too forceful a personality, and had too definite ideas of his own, to reflect very faithfully the conditions around him, and the average reader feels this very easily. But Tchekov seems to be endowed with a passivity which is peculiarly Russian itself, part of the oriental mentality, and which Tchekov himself has portrayed so admirably in so many figures. One cannot help feeling that a man of this kind, possessed of such a faculty for doing nothing, for passive experience, must have been admirably suited to give a true account of what was going on round about him. Further, the general picture which he presents in his plays is so completely consistent with that given in his stories. Altogether, he has left us a picture of such complexity that we feel he could not have invented it, at any rate not with such perfect consistency. And, as a part of this picture, his plays seem to me to be as near the ideal of realism as plays possibly can be. Even allowing for the initial difficulty of the language, and for the fact that we have only a literary notion of the life of Russians, I am prepared to trust my sensibility in this; Tchekov's whole personality, the atmosphere of his plays, the way in which they are constructed—everything about him confirms my feeling that he is the writer who has most nearly conformed with the ideal of realism. Above all, his pessimism, his attitude to life, seems to be not so much his own as a part of the normal outlook of the people represented in his plays, the decadent and unhappy Russian bourgeoisie; and so we feel no surprise when they give expression to it—it is their natural method of talking.

Apart from Tchekov, we have the plays of Tolstoy, which are not among his best work, and which show a certain clumsiness in the management of dramatic form which robs them of any realism which they might otherwise have. Of Gogol, I know only one comedy, *Marriage*, which is charming in its way, but is not particularly realistic—perhaps it is too amusing for that. Turgenieff's *Month in the Country* is largely an anticipation of Tchekov, and all that we have said of Tchekov will be true of it.

And so we come to the Scandinavians, Ibsen and Strindberg. With them, there is the same difficulty as with the Russians, in an even more acute form, because we rely for our impression of the life of the people represented only on the plays themselves; there are no novels or short stories to help us, as there are with the Russians. In short, we have no standard at all by which to measure the realism of either of these writers, and must rely entirely on general impressions.

In the case of Strindberg we have a standard of reference in the comparison of the plays one with another. In his first period of creative activity, he wrote historical plays which are excellent of their kind (*Master Olof* especially) and which certainly possess that peculiar realism which we have ascribed to the historical drama. In the eighties, however, he came under the influence of the French school, and the result, especially in the plays *The Father* and *Lady Julia*, was the achievement of true realism, and true drama. Here Strindberg's peculiar gift was his extraordinarily acute feeling for the reactions between people, especially those that cannot ordinarily be expressed in words, but which are often so much more vivid and significant than anything in more concrete form. In this middle period, this gift was present, certainly, but in a reasonable degree, and it rather serves to augment the effect of realism which he attains. Indeed, in this particular respect, Strindberg has no equal: he attains a kind of realism which is found nowhere else.

But later in life, when he had passed through spiritual crises which brought him very near to insanity, this same gift became exaggerated out of all proportion, and he developed a sort of hyper-aesthesia in the feeling for personal relations which is very comparable with Van Gogh's hardly sane hyper-aesthesia for colour and for sunlight. Probably it was owing to this very quality in his social reactions that Strindberg suffered so much in his relations with other people, and especially with his unfortunate wives. And certainly it was the extreme development of it which made him turn from realism in his work to that peculiar kind of drama which is still all his own;—drama in which the reactions between people are portrayed with terrible fidelity, but by methods which diverge ever more from realism, and which depend on the expression of feelings so subtle that they are never, in real life, put into the form of words. *The Ghost Sonata* is perhaps the best example of this type of work, and in it we can see how Strindberg was evolving a method of symbolical representation which is the very reverse of realism. Compared with plays like this, we may safely judge the work of the middle period to be truly realistic, and, of its particular kind, uniquely so, through the possession of this uncanny social faculty.

The case of Ibsen is in some ways not unlike that of Strindberg. Ibsen too commenced his career with some admirable historical plays, and passed from them, through the more obviously poetical period of *Peer Gynt* and *Brand*, to a realistic middle period, in such plays as *The League of Youth*, *Pillars of Society*, *A Doll's House* and *Ghosts*. All these are models of realism, and in their own way—though that is a way different from Tchekov or Strindberg—as near to the ideal of the realists as drama can be.

One aspect of these plays deserves special attention. They are all, at first sight, concerned with problems of a sociological nature, dealing with the condition of society, with marriage, the emancipation of women, and kindred subjects. They are, in fact, apparently not unlike the plays of Bernard Shaw and Brieux.[1] But a closer examination will reveal certain fundamental

---

[1] I take these writers merely as examples of their kind. Everything that I may say of them will be true of any other drama of the didactic, sociological kind—for example of the plays of Mr Somerset Maugham.

differences. To Shaw, and to writers like him, these sociological problems are treated in a scientific, a genuinely scientific, way; that is to say, the dramatist himself is *altruistically*, not *personally*, interested in them. Ibsen, on the other hand, was directly and personally interested in the problems with which he deals. For him, they were not abstract problems, but questions upon which his own way of living and feeling depended directly. In a word, Ibsen was a poet, and Shaw is not a poet, but a very able dramatic sociologist and politician.

Ibsen once wrote: "Everything that I have written has the closest possible connection with what I have lived through, even if it has not been my own personal experience; in every new poem or play, I have aimed at my own spiritual emancipation and purification".

Certainly this is far from the attitude of Shaw, who has been concerned less with his own salvation than with the salvation of England. Ibsen too was concerned, in a way, with the salvation of Norway, but only because it was inextricably bound up with his own salvation.

One might expect, in view of this difference between them, that Shaw's work would be more realistic than Ibsen's—that it would be more scientific, more objective, more faithful to life. But actually the reverse is the case. And the reason is, that men differ much more in their opinions than in their feelings. Shaw, expounding a particular theory on the slum-question, is dealing with a matter which is, after all, temporary; and he deals with it in a temporary way, leaving out, as far as he can, his own more profound reactions to the whole problem of evil which it implicates. Ibsen, if he had dealt with the same subject, would have turned it into a matter of pure personal feeling, not of abstract justice: would have probed the problem of evil in society, and of the attitude of the individual to it. And in doing so, he would have reached a stratum of human experience which does not depend on opinion, on fashion, or any temporary and contingent circumstance, but which is a sort of highest common factor of human experience. It is because experience of this kind is common to all men, because all men can enter into it, as something very near to their own lives, that Ibsen is, and always will be, more realistic than Shaw, whose realism, already impaired by the too frequent appearance of the author behind the masks of his characters, will almost disappear when the subjects with which he deals have passed out of fashion.

In a word, Ibsen shows us that the highest realism in the drama, as in all art, depends on the greatest imagination, on the highest poetic faculty, which apprehends its own personal problems with such profundity that they are transformed into universal problems, which every man can understand and feel as his own.[1] So, in a much more subtle sense than Aristotle's, the characters of such drama will be "just like ourselves".

In this profound imaginative ability for elevating his own moral problems and the moral problems of the society in which he lived, to a universal, mythological level, Ibsen resembles Aeschylus more than any other dramatist. Aeschylus was concerned always with the conflict of two systems of morality, two attitudes to life. The one, represented by the Eumenides, was the old, crude, barbaric morality of the early

[1] How much of Ibsen's poetry we lose simply through translation, I do not know. But at least we should take care to remember—a thing that we often forget—that his countrymen always regarded him as a *poet*, and that his biographers refer to him always by that name.

Greeks. The other was the morality of Apollo, enlightened, civilised.[1] The conflict between the two is to be found in all society, and Ibsen found it very clearly in Norway, setting himself, as Aeschylus had done, on the side of Apollo. We may quote an excellent passage of Dr Brandes:

Even Mrs Alving, who has been so sorely wronged by circumstances, believes that under other conditions she might have been happy, believes that her wretched husband himself might have been happy. And Ibsen is evidently of her opinion. What she says about the "half-grown town" that has "no joys to offer, only dissipations, no object in life, only an official position, no real work, only business", comes from Ibsen's heart. Life itself is not an evil. Existence itself is not joyless. No, some one is to blame, or rather many are to blame, when a life is lost to the joy of life; and Norwegian society, depressing, coarse in its pleasures, enslaved to conventional ideas of duty, is pointed to as the culprit.[2]

Professor Saintsbury has complained that Ibsen was "parochial"; rather, he is, with Aeschylus, the great opponent of parochiality, urging humanity, and his own country, to leave

[1] This aspect of the work of Aeschylus has been admirably studied by Professor Ridgeway, in *The Origins of Greek Tragedy*.

[2] Second impression of Ibsen, English translation, p. 52.

[116]

barbarism, and to enter upon the morality and life of enlightenment. And in doing so, he achieved the highest kind of realism, fulfilling the ideals of the particular school which we have been discussing, and doing much more besides.

In his later plays, Ibsen diverges from the realistic model more frankly in the direction of poetry, and employs symbolism, with other completely unrealistic devices, just as Strindberg was doing at the same time. With the middle period of these two poets, the great period of realism reached its climax, and with their passing on to a new form of drama, it came to an end as a separate kind of writing.

Two things we should add here. Firstly, that in Tchekov, Strindberg, and Ibsen, we find the pessimism which we have described as the characteristic of realism, in Tchekov tempered and moderate, in Strindberg violent and exaggerated, and in Ibsen profound and philosophic.[1]

Secondly, it is clear that to a great extent, all these dramatists were free from the notions of

---

[1] Ibsen was actually much influenced by the Dane Soren Kierkegaard, one of the most profound philosophers of the nineteenth century, who expressed a pessimism of a very original kind.

tragedy and comedy in the Aristotelian sense. They do not represent the deaths of Kings and Princes (except in their historical plays, of course), nor the heroic struggles which delighted the Elizabethan audience. It is a far cry from the "tragic deaths" of Hamlet, Coriolanus, Brutus, Anthony, and the rest, or even of Arden, to the quiet passing away of the old servant in *The Cherry Orchard*, the girl behind the screen in Strindberg's *The Ghost Sonata*, and the peaceful, almost symbolic deaths which characterise Ibsen's later plays.

The practice of realism, then, sufficiently confirms the view of it which we have reached on theoretical grounds. It remains for us to attempt a conclusion.

CONCLUSION

Wto real life as close as is compatible with the
nature of dramatic illusion. Its chief formal
characteristic is that it takes characters which are
as far as possible just like ourselves, and so falls
between the categories of tragedy and comedy,
as defined by Aristotle. Like any other drama,
but not more than any other drama, it must be
constructed according to the circumstances of
the stage and of the theatre. But we must inter-
pret these circumstances liberally, remembering
what the Neo-Classics on the whole forgot, that
the audience has a definite preconception of the
drama, and that any extensive deviation from the
accepted practice will tend to diminish the effect
of realism.

In a more specific sense, as applied to a school
of drama in the last century, the usage of the
word need not be distinguished from its general
sense as sharply as we might have supposed.

CONCLUSION

Formally, at any rate, the works of this school do not seem to be very different from the works of earlier periods. And the chief thing which distinguishes them from their predecessors is their use of a particular attitude which became common in Europe at that time—pessimism. We have endeavoured to show why pessimism should produce realism.

Thus our conclusion is perhaps not a very striking one: that a certain amount of realism is to be found in all periods of the drama, and that it is not the particular asset of any one period or school. I am well aware that if we had adopted another mode of inquiry, we might have arrived at very different results. If we had considered only the so-called realist school, we should probably have found reason to believe that it was unique and remarkable: we should have been able to make it into a new category of art. In some ways, that might have been more interesting, but I doubt whether it would have been more useful. Criticism of that kind, as we have said in our introduction, generally results in the kind of definition which is a hindrance to the creative artist. Historical criticism, on the other hand, is concerned rather with the abolition of definitions. This it should achieve by relating past definitions with the past, by relegating them, in fact, to a sort of museum of critical terms which have no further use. This at any rate leaves the creative impulse of the dramatist free and un-hampered, as it should be. And if anyone were to ask me "How shall I write a realistic play?", I can only answer, "Write as you please. Have a due consideration for the circumstances of the theatre, and above all for the natural preconception of the drama which your audience will have. But beyond that, there are no technical devices which will help you, and only by a complete sincerity with yourself will you be able to reach a kind of human experience which is common to all men, which will be felt by your audience to be a part of themselves, so that they will have the impression, at least, that your characters are, indeed, just like themselves."

For EU product safety concerns, contact us at Calle de José Abascal, 56–1°,
28003 Madrid, Spain or eugpsr@cambridge.org.